the
naturescaping
workbook

the

naturescaping

workbook

A Step-by-Step Guide for Bringing Nature to Your Backyard

BY Beth O'Donnell Young

WITH PHOTOGRAPHS BY Karen Bussolini

Timber Press

PORTLAND / LONDON

Published in 2011 by Timber Press, Inc.

The Haseltine Building
133 S.W. Second Avenue, Suite 450
Portland, Oregon 97204-3527
www.timberpress.com

2 The Quadrant
135 Salusbury Road
London NW6 6RJ
www.timberpress.co.uk

Printed in China
Design by Nicki Brandt

Library of Congress Cataloging-in-Publication Data
Young, Beth O'Donnell.
The naturescaping workbook: a step-by-step guide for
bringing nature to your backyard/Beth O'Donnell Young;
with photographs by Karen Bussolini—1st ed.
p. cm.
Includes bibliographical references and index.
ISBN 978-1-60469-118-4
1. Natural landscaping. 2. Natural gardens—Design. I. Bussolini, Karen.
II. Title. III. Title: A step-by-step guide for bringing nature to your backyard.
SB439.Y68 2011
635.9'5—dc22
2011012385

A catalog record for this book is also available from the British Library.

❧ TO MY PARENTS ☙

John and Shirley O'Donnell
with love and gratitude

contents

WORKSHEETS

When you visit your local natural areas often, you will learn to design like nature. In this near-to-natural garden, a flowering redbud heralds the beginning of spring, just like in the surrounding foothills. Design by Ana Hajduk.

acknowledgments

My parents gave me love and encouragement and always told me—and my three sisters—that we could do anything we set our minds to do. Mother said I was beautiful, strong, and complicated, but she is all that and so much more. Dad has always been proud of me; I can see it in his eyes when he looks at me.

Teresa Matteson of the Benton Soil and Water Conservation District, Tom Kaye of the Institute for Applied Ecology, Jeff Picton of Chintimini Wildlife Center, James Cassidy of the Oregon State University (OSU) Department of Crop and Soil Science, Bill Proebesting and Tom Cook of the OSU Department of Horticulture (both retired), Mark Taratoot of the City of Corvallis, Linda McMahan of the OSU Extension Service, writer and wildlife gardener Lisa Albert, and professional hydrologist Chip Andrus generously volunteered to share their expertise with the students in my "Naturescape Your Yard" classes; they are gems and I consider them coauthors of this book. Colin Gillin, president of the American Association of Wildlife Veterinarians, and Jeff Gillman of the University of Minnesota Department of Horticultural Science each gave me quick and accurate technical advice whenever I asked.

The citizens of Corvallis, Oregon, who signed up for my "Naturescape Your Yard" classes affirmed my hunch that people want to learn about how to work with nature. Without their enthusiasm and positive feedback, this book simply would not exist.

Lorraine Anderson suggested that we write a gardening book together and helped me get the book deal with Timber Press, then became the developmental editor and drafted the introduction to this book. If I am the mother of this book, Lorraine is the godmother.

Toby Hemenway, Rose Marie Nichols McGee, Scott Calhoun, William L. Sullivan, Paul Tukey, and Ella Mae Wolff generously and graciously shared with me their insights as published authors of nature and garden books.

Karen Bussolini, who I knew would be the perfect photographer for this book when I first saw a photo of her, arms brimming with gifts from the garden, became a fast friend in the course of our first phone conversation.

Bill Young, a very talented amateur photographer as well as a good man and a good friend, took on an eleventh-hour photography assignment with enthusiasm and extreme professionalism.

To all these people who have made this book possible, I offer my gratitude and appreciation—and to you, the reader, for having faith in me that I can teach you how to understand and enjoy your land.

THE NATURESCAPING WAY

Imagine working in concert with nature to create an inviting, lush, healthy landscape that rarely needs weeding, pruning, watering, fertilizing, or mowing—in short, one that requires less time, money, and energy than you are probably spending on your garden right now. Imagine knowing that your yard is contributing to the peace of your neighborhood, safeguarding the health of local streams and rivers, keeping the air cleaner, and inviting songbirds and frogs and bees to return.

This is the promise of naturescaping, and it's within reach of everyone who has a plot of land to work, whether a postage stamp in the city or acres upon acres in the countryside.

What is Naturescaping?

Naturescaping is a new yet very old way of landscaping. It is a quiet revolution in the way we garden based on a growing awareness of our interrelationship with all of life. It's thinking in terms of restoring our own backyard ecosystems. It's allowing natural cycles and processes to work without interference. It's making intelligent use of resources by conserving water, using organic material generated on-site to improve the nutrient and physical structure of soil, and using local, recycled, and low-impact building materials where called for. It's choosing native and appropriate plant species in groupings adapted to the spot where we place them, and making a welcoming habitat for wildlife. It's working with, instead of against, nature to minimize the amount of time and energy required for maintenance. It's being mindful of the impact of our choices on the wider world beyond our own backyards.

The term *naturescaping* first sprouted in an Oregon Department of Fish and Wildlife publication in the early 1990s and has since poked up shoots all over the country. By 2007 an entry for *naturescaping* had appeared in Wikipedia. The idea has been around for longer, though, and has gone by different names. It borrows concepts and consciousness from permaculture, a system of designing sustainable human settlements worked out by Bill Mollison and David Holmgren of the University of Tasmania in the 1970s and since refined around the world. The Sunset Western Garden Book calls it gardening for the new century. The U.S. Environmental Protection Agency prefers the term *greenscaping*. The Ecological Landscaping Association, formed in 1992, labels it—what else?—ecological landscaping. Others have called it design with nature and sustainable landscaping.

However it's labeled and no matter who's advocating it, naturescaping is based on the realization that our current landscaping and gardening practices are harmful to our soil, our rivers, our air, and every living creature, including us. Something has to change.

In my garden design business, I work with homeowners in creating landscape plans for their yards. In 2005 I decided to create a class called "Naturescape Your Yard" because I realized that many of my clients did not know the basics of plant growth and natural ecosystems. They would ask me, "How far should I cut this back?" or "What should I spray on that?" as if their gardens were naughty children who needed constant correction or terminally ill patients in need of toxic chemicals to stay alive. This was not due to lack of formal education (most of my clients are college-educated); they simply didn't know any other way to garden.

For some reason we no longer look to nature to provide for us, even in our gardens. We populate our gardens with plants from other parts of the world and struggle to keep them alive with fertilizers and extra water—even pesticides. We take away organic material from our yards and then, because our soil is weak and exposed, add topsoil, fertilizers, and ground covers. When we are not setting ourselves up for failure, we are setting ourselves up for a lifetime of boring yardwork.

By contrast, a naturescaped backyard is a place that teems with life and health, wastes nothing, and thrives on just what's offered by its soil and climate. It's a lively outdoor space, full of bugs and birds, that nourishes our great hunger to be in contact with nature while it contributes at the same time to the health of our earth. Working in a naturescape is not a chore; it is a labor of love.

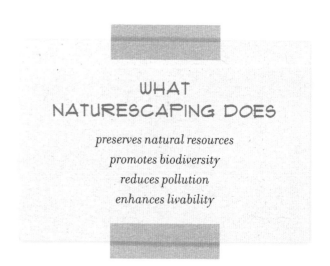

WHAT NATURESCAPING DOES

preserves natural resources
promotes biodiversity
reduces pollution
enhances livability

Naturescaped yards are lush, inviting, and naturally low-care.

NATURESCAPING PRINCIPLES

LET'S BEGIN WITH A SET OF PRINCIPLES THAT ARE AT THE CORE OF NATURESCAPING. THEY ANSWER A KEY QUESTION: WHAT WOULD NATURE DO? EACH OF THE CHAPTERS THAT FOLLOW WILL TAKE UP ONE OF THESE PRINCIPLES.

1. Get to know your place on earth before altering it in any way.

2. Manage runoff and reduce your need for supplementary water to protect local waterways and water supplies.

3. Put the right plant in the right place, based on function, needs, and natural communities.

4. Attract birds, small animals, an beneficial insects by providing welcoming habitat and rely on them to do the pest patrol.

5. Choose materials that are environmentally sustainable for the built elements of your garden.

6. Let nature be your guide as you put design decisions on paper.

7. Think in terms of whole systems as you install your naturescape, from clearing the land to planting and mulching.

8. Continue to build your soil with organic matter as you maintain your naturescape, for fewer pests and diseases, less watering, and less work.

In this Northwest garden, a planting of drought-tolerant Japanese barberry, black-eyed Susans, and ornamental grasses offers year-round interest and needs little maintenance. Caution: Japanese barberry is listed as invasive in some states.

A naturescape promotes biodiversity and enhances livability by including space for homegrown fruits and vegetables.

Why Naturescape Your Yard?

Why naturescape? Because it saves you time and money. Because it feeds your soul as much as your soil. Because it protects our beautiful home planet. Naturescaping can save you money. Chemical pesticides, herbicides, and fertilizers are expensive, as are huge quantities of water. If you are converting a conventional landscape, it will cost you up front to replace what you already have, but you'll save on water, fertilizer, mowing, yard help, pesticides, topsoil, and plant-replacement costs over the years.

A naturescaped yard can even reduce your home energy costs. Properly chosen and positioned trees and shrubs can reduce—or eliminate—the need for air conditioning by shading your home in summer. Deciduous trees and shrubs can reduce your winter heating costs by allowing winter's warming rays to get to your house, while more distant evergreen trees and shrubs can act as windbreaks.

More subtle but just as real is the fact that you will get enjoyment out of your naturescape. When you begin to think like nature, to cooperate with nature, to learn from nature, your backyard will cease being a time-and-money sink and become a space where you can connect deeply with the beauty, health, and peace of nature. You can recharge there after the stress and struggle of everyday life, you can fill all your senses, you can feel truly alive and glad to be part of an abundant universe. Your inner world becomes richer as your outer garden blooms.

And, of course, there is that satisfying feeling that you are doing your part to restore health and vitality to the land you have been entrusted with. This may not seem significant when viewed from a global scale, but it is. Each naturescaped yard gives back to its larger ecological systems much more than it takes. And as more and more of us start naturescaping, the benefits to the earth will compound.

❧ **Nature develops landscapes over eons, perfectly suited to the conditions prevailing in the place.** Get to know your place on earth—its weathers and seasons, plants and animals, soil and drainage patterns, natural and human history, natural processes, design challenges and opportunities—before altering it in any way.

❧ **Nature encourages atmospheric water (rainwater or snowmelt) to soak into the ground where it falls. Nature plants species where they'll survive with the amount of water provided.** Manage runoff and reduce your need for supplementary water to protect local waterways and water supplies.

❧ **In nature, plants grow where they can thrive with the soil, moisture, and light provided, in ordered, long-lived, self-sustaining communities or guilds where each plays an ecological role and may serve many purposes.** Put the right plant in the right place, based on function, needs, and natural communities.

❧ **Nature works toward equilibrium with predator and prey species. Pests are kept in check by natural enemies.** Attract birds, small animals, and beneficial insects by providing a welcoming habitat and rely on them to do the pest patrol.

❧ **Nature incorporates native wood, stone, gravel, and other materials into landscapes.** Choose materials that are environmentally sustainable for the built elements of your garden.

❧ **In nature, woodlands, meadows, and watercourses occur where natural conditions are right for them.** Let nature be your guide as you put design decisions on paper.

❧ **Nature builds soil by accumulating organic debris on the soil surface and breaking it down from the top. Nature does not till, dig, rake, mow, or use a leafblower. It allows leaves and dead branches to decompose where they fall.** There are no weeds. Think in terms of whole systems as you install your naturescape, from clearing the land to planting and mulching. Continue to build your soil with organic matter for fewer pests and diseases, less watering, and less work.

These basic principles form the foundation of naturescaping. Keep them in mind as you make choices at each step in the design process.

How to Use This Book

Whether your starting point is an old landscape that needs total renovation, a new backyard consisting of nothing but yards of dirt, or something in between, this book offers you a step-by-step process for designing and installing your naturescape. You will encounter questionnaires, worksheets, and instructions on how to gather different types of information that will serve as design inputs. You may want to keep this material all together in a binder, folder, or portfolio to document your design process. Downloadable pdfs of the worksheets are available at my website, http://www.naturescapeyouryard.com.

Chapter 1 focuses your attention on thoroughly assessing your place on earth and what you already have in your backyard. Don't expect to do this in a hurry; ideally, you would closely observe your yard over the course of an entire year before making any move to alter it. During this time you can gather ideas from everywhere, from the garden down the street or the state park an hour's drive away.

Chapters 2 through 5 focus on choices you'll need to make regarding water, plants, wildlife habitat, and durable materials to be used in your garden. These chapters challenge you to think in terms of ecological systems—that is, in terms of the interactions among living organisms that are continuously happening on your little piece of the earth's surface and in relation to its surroundings. They provide information that will help you think through the broader impact of your decisions.

Then in chapter 6 you will turn to drawing up the design, followed in chapter 7 by installing your naturescape and in chapter 8 by continuing to build the soil as you maintain your new garden.

Recognizing that you may be more or less comfortable with plants and landscaping, this book aims to give you basic steps and steer you toward additional resources to make it easier for you. Some naturescaping concepts and practices will likely go against everything you've been taught. It takes courage to be different. But I think you'll be more than satisfied with the results as your naturescape gains health and vitality with each passing year and practically takes care of itself, allowing you to enjoy the fruits of your labors.

*A naturescape blends into its natural surroundings and could have been designed by nature,
like this woodland garden in Connecticut.* Design by Natureworks.

A NATURESCAPING MAKEOVER

When Lorraine Anderson bought her town-house with large backyard in May 2006, the garden was, shall we say, pure potential. Between rotting, leaning fences stretched nothing but a vast green expanse of lawn. The previous owner had no doubt succumbed to a weekly or biweekly ritual of firing up the power mower and roaring up and down, disturbing the weekend silence. The summer months of dragging the sprinkler all over the place and pouring gallons of water on the lawn were probably followed by fall and spring applications of weed-and-feed. And for all this effort, there was a soul-deadening monotony to the landscape—a landscape visited only by raucous blue jays and occasional possums, and otherwise devoid of wildlife.

Lorraine enrolled in my first "Naturescape Your Yard" class through the local environmental center. She spent the first four months in her new home peeling back and cutting away yards and yards of black plastic sheeting that had been laid down decades before under bark chips. (The tacky stuff had long since stopped suppressing weeds, which were smart enough to grow in the layer of decomposed organic matter on top of the plastic.) When the ground could breathe again she forked in some of the accumulated layers of decomposed leaves from the trees overhead.

She graded the soil under the front deck to slope away from—rather than toward, as it had been—the foundation and dug a triangular hole next to the deck measuring roughly a yard on each side and a foot and a half deep. In this "rain garden" (created to collect storm water so it could slowly percolate into the ground) she planted water-loving sedges and reeds, and backfilled with small smooth rocks she found under an old woodpile. She had a portion of her entry path replaced to correct its unfortunate slope toward the foundation and used the broken-up concrete (known in the recycling world as urbanite) to make a low retaining wall.

After watching for months how the sun tracked through the sky overhead, drawing a map of the backyard, and, as she put it, "messing around endlessly" with ideas on tracing paper, she got down to work. The lawn had grown knee high and turned brown, presenting a fire hazard. By hand she whacked back and raked up the dead grass and piled it on top of flattened cardboard boxes she had laid down where new beds would be. She reduced the lawn area to about a sixth of its former size. She began excavating for a small patio and piled the rocky clay soil on top of the cardboard boxes and dead grass. With a square-nosed shovel she also stripped the sod from areas that would be paths and heaved these rugs of grass upside down onto the planting beds. She built two compost bins from pallets scrounged from behind a local store.

While waiting for her own compost to ripen, she topped all the beds with compost from a local landscape supply place and started planting a mix of native and appropriate plants. She made a colorful drought-tolerant perennial bed anchored with a mix of evergreen and deciduous shrubs and also created a cutting-flower bed, a strawberry bed, a blueberry bed, an herb bed, three vegetable beds, and thick "habitat" borders where native evergreen screening shrubs would grow up to give privacy on all sides of the yard. She planted a 'Forest Pansy' redbud tree for color and shade by the patio, and an aspen grove in the back corner for the swishy sound of quaking leaves to cover traffic noise. For carefree ornamental edibles, she planted a persimmon tree, a fig tree in a large pot, and two pineapple guava shrubs.

After about a year, Lorraine had a yard that was well on its way back to health. By that spring, black-capped chickadees, cedar waxwings, finches, robins, and hummingbirds had begun visiting, and ladybugs were everywhere. The vista from the living room windows encompassed bright pink blossoms forming on native red-flowering currant, leaves unfurling on drought-tolerant chokeberry bushes, lavenders and yarrows beginning to form blooms, red-twig dogwoods giving hints of leaves to come, and the branches of vine maple, Pacific wax myrtle, and coast silk tassel stretching eagerly upward. Weeds pulled easily from soil that was developing body and tilth. The garden had begun to feel right, no longer an impoverished and overcontrolled piece of ground but a yard full of life.

A patio edged with river stones, coneflower and coreopsis, fountain grass and taller 'Karl Foerster' feather reed grass, and a 'Forest Pansy' redbud tree has replaced one corner of a boring expanse of lawn in Lorraine Anderson's naturescape.

chapter one

KNOW YOUR PLACE

Get to know your place on earth before altering it in any way.

All too often, gardens are designed without an awareness of the natural patterns and processes of the land. An obvious and common example is a new patio added off of the kitchen or dining room without any regard to the sun exposure. I've visited my share of never-used concrete patios on the west side of the house where every summer afternoon the sun blasts, making the area feel more like a fireplace than a restful oasis.

Close observation of your nearby ecosystems, such as how densely nature "planted" these trees, will make you a better naturescaper.

The easiest way to discover nature's patterns and processes is observation over a good period of time—ideally, a full year or more. Observe your yard, your neighborhood, and your nearby natural ecosystems. Observe the weathers and seasons, plants and animals, soil and drainage patterns, natural and human history, natural processes, and design challenges and opportunities of your place on earth and your particular piece of land. Observe yourself and your family and think about what you really want out of your naturescape, now and in the future.

To some, patient observation might seem a daunting task. After all, we live in a fast-paced world and we seldom have or make the time to just slow down and observe. But as beloved garden writer Gertrude Jekyll wrote in *Children and Gardens*: "One of the best ways to be happy is be observant." When you learn to simply listen to and observe nature, you will become comfortable with letting the land itself make a great majority of your design decisions.

Start with What You Have

Start the naturescape design process by carefully examining just what you already have on your land. Take note of existing structures, including your house, and find out something about their history. Tune into views and noise, and how these change with the seasons. Notice slopes and drainage patterns, and see where water tends to pool during winter months. Check out patterns of sun, shade, and wind in all four seasons. Locate utilities and drain fields. Observe the impact of neighbors, both human and wild, on your yard. And become familiar with local laws, codes, and regulations that might affect your design decisions.

During this stage of the design process, taking notes and photographs can be a great help. A worksheet is provided here to guide your observation and prompt your note taking. You might want to make a copy of it and keep it in a naturescaping binder, folder, or portfolio.

WORKSHEET 1: WHAT I ALREADY HAVE

OVERVIEW

What would you say are the problem areas of your property?

What are the functional problems with your property?
(Example: when it's raining you get wet when you take out the garbage.)

Are there features on your property, man-made or otherwise, that you would like to remove?

Are there any natural features on your property that you would like to emphasize or enhance (such as an existing pond or stream)?

Are there any areas where nothing grows?

What would you say are the best features of your property?

EXISTING STRUCTURES

What year was your house built?

What is the style?

What is the square footage?

What are the façade materials?

What is the paint color, now or in the near future?

What other structures exist on your land?

YOUR PROPERTY'S HISTORY

What is the history of your property before the house was built?

Do you know the history of your land since the house was built, such as use of pesticides (versus organic methods of pest control), or if the land was heavily mulched?

VIEWS AND NOISE

What are the visual problems with your property?

What are the most important views from inside your house?

Are there good views from your property that you want enhanced?

Are there poor views that you want blocked?

Is noise a problem anywhere on your site?

SLOPES AND DRAINAGE PATTERNS

Are there any slopes on your land?

Are there any rock outcrops on your land?

Do your paved areas drain away from your house's foundation adequately?

Do you have any lawn areas or planting beds that get mucky or have seasonal standing water?

Where do your downspouts drain to: pipes and gutters, or a drainage swale?

Where does your driveway drain to?

What is your water source: city or well?

PATTERNS OF SUN, SHADE, AND WIND

What are the seasonal sun and shade patterns?

Which areas are almost always shady?

Where are your sun pockets (spots that are usually warmer than the surrounding areas)?

Are there areas that get too hot in the summer?

What is the prevailing wind direction, if any? Is wind a problem?

What are your annual temperature highs and lows?

UTILITIES AND DRAIN FIELDS

Are there any municipal or utility easements on your property?

Any underground utility lines?

Any drain fields?

YOUR NEIGHBORS, HUMAN AND WILD

Are there any chronic activities of your immediate neighbors that might affect your naturescape design?

Do your neighbors have concerns that you should take into consideration?

What kind of wildlife, if any, visits your yard?

LOCAL LAWS, CODES, AND REGULATIONS

Do any municipal or county codes affect what you can do on your land?

Are there any CC&R's that might affect your design decisions?

Existing structures and your property's history

How old is your house? Think about how the house—and the surrounding community—has looked over the decades of its life. What was the land like before the house was built? Was it farmland? What sort of farm? And try to picture the land before any human development. Would it have been an open field? A forest? A desert? Thinking in these terms, and perhaps a little library research, will help you to understand your land in a deeper way and might suggest design themes to you.

Views and noise

Walk around your land with new eyes. Notice distant things, such as a neighbor's majestic tree with beautiful fall color. Maybe you will want a path to curve so that all of a sudden, the walker gets an eyeful of that tree in all its glory. Or perhaps you will want to choose some shrubs with that same fall color, repeating and enhancing this beautiful specimen.

One of my landscape design clients had a yard that backed onto a busy rural road. Beyond the road, however, were rolling foothills of grass (a grass-seed farm) with a distant ribbon of ash trees and big-leaf maples: a creek wending though the fields. A white farmhouse tucked into the trees gave this lovely tableau a picturesque focal point. The former owners had placed a 6-foot fence on their property line, blocking both the road and the view. Luckily, the roadway was sunken about 3 feet below the land on either side, so the new homeowner needed only a 3-1/2-foot fence to maintain privacy yet let in that fantastic view.

Notice visual problems with your property as well. Do the neighbor's second-story windows look down into your back garden, denying you privacy? Does an unsightly wall, street sign, or fence degrade the visual harmony of your front yard? As you look around your land, pay attention to the visual disharmony that you may have become accustomed to. Luckily, most visual problems can be solved with the precise placement of the right plant: a tall evergreen can block your neighbor's view into your yard, a lacy vine can break up an uninteresting wall, and a mixed border of shrubs and perennials can make street signage or ugly fencing virtually disappear.

And noise. The funny thing about noise—even traffic noise—is that people get used to it. I've walked into a backyard that sounded like a freeway and piped up, "Oh, you must hate the noise back here," only to be met with blank stares; they had not noticed. But if any noise bothers *you*, take heart. Your naturescape can incorporate elements that help mask the sound—walls and fences, of course, but also large plants and ones that give off swishy sounds. How about using the wind or rain in creative ways to make sound?

The style of your house might help you make some landscape design decisions. This house is in the Arts and Crafts style of the early twentieth century, a style characterized by grids interlaced with naturalistic patterns, which suggested formal beds softened by exuberant prairielike plantings. Design by Natureworks.

This naturescape borrows a view of fields, trees, and distant blue hills beyond the low back fence Design by Beth Young Garden Design, LLC.

PHOTOGRAPH YOUR YARD

In this digital world, you cannot take too many "before" photos of your yard. Your photographs will reveal your house's details and its relationship to your land as well as give you a good overview of your yard and its surroundings. Plus years from now you will enjoy the satisfaction of comparing your current naturescape with the way your yard used to look.

Store your digital photos on a computer that you can access while you are working on the design drawings later on. A laptop set up next to your drawing surface is great for this but not strictly needed; simply having the computer in the same room will be fine. Once in a while you might want to print out a photo, so having a color printer linked to that computer would be helpful.

If you are using traditional photography methods, have your photos printed out as 5x7s with a matte finish. Before I went digital, I found it helpful to tape the photos to the wall next to my drafting board while I was working on the design. Afterward they can be stored in your naturescaping folder or binder.

Here is a systematic way to take photos of your yard:

1. Photograph each wall of your house from two angles. For example, if you start with the south wall, stand at the southwest corner of the house and take a shot of the south wall (and while you are there, take a shot of the west wall). Stand where you can get the entire wall in one or two shots. Now move to the SE corner of the house and do the same. Go around the house doing this. These shots will record doors, windows, downspouts, water faucets, cracks and unsightly spots, and so on.

2. Photograph the yard and the house from a distance. This time you will stand at, or outside, your property lines so as to get some panoramic shots. Again, take photos from each corner—SW, SE, NE, NW—and shoot toward the house. These shots will capture the house and its visual relationship with the land, surrounding trees, and other landscape features.

3. Photograph the surrounding landscape from the house. To do this, stand at the center of the house and take a series of photos from left to right encompassing the entire yard. These shots give an overview of the yard as well as vistas you may want to hide or accentuate.

4. Photograph key areas. This might be a gate, the way a path meets the sidewalk, or anything else that you want to make a visual note of. It could also be a view that you know you will want to have a "before" photo of because you have an idea that you know will change that view.

Most cameras cannot take photos that are wide enough to show your entire property in one shot; you will have to piece together such a shot yourself. If you are using a digital camera you might want to use a software program—usually called something like "panorama maker"—to join your photos. To prepare for the panorama maker, taking the shots from left to right makes the photos a lot easier to handle. If you are using a traditional camera, you will need to manually cut and tape together your photos.

The trick to panoramas is to have some overlap, but not too much. That is, on your first photograph, note something, perhaps a tree trunk, that is about a quarter of the photo's width from the right edge of the photo. For the next photo, move the camera to the right until that tree trunk is a quarter of the photo's width from the left edge, and take that shot, and so on.

In this age of digital photography, you can never take too many "before" photographs.

Slopes and drainage patterns

The slope of your land affects everything from sun exposure to moisture retention. It determines if you will be needing steps or ramps, or if terracing would help. For now, you might just want to walk around your property and note the general slope of the land, if any.

Now is also the time to notice if your yard has any seasonally mucky areas, areas that never dry out, or areas that become impromptu rivers when it rains. Conventional landscape solutions to these situations include diverting the water to a dry well or creating a French drain. A naturescaping solution is to accept that you have wet conditions and populate that area with plants that thrive in the muck. For now, being aware of these spots is all that is needed. Also note any existing natural features such as ponds or streams that you would like to preserve or enhance.

Take note of where your downspouts and driveway drain to. Most local codes dictate that all water that lands on your property must filter into your soil or be taken away in the sanitary sewer system. In other words, "your" water should not flow overland to your neighbor's yard (with the exception of an established creek or river).

Patterns of sun, shade, and wind

It's important to know the sun and shade patterns in your yard, not just in the summer but all year long. How does the sun track over your property in the winter compared to the summer? I live on the 45th parallel so the summer sun really beats on my west-facing walls for many hours, much more than it did when I lived in the San Francisco Bay Area, parallel 37. But every winter up here in Oregon at 45, the sun is weak, far away; a distant arc that might warm a south-facing wall only a little, if at all. Knowing how—and how hard—the sun hits the various parts of your yard through the seasons will help you to make good plant choices later.

If wind is a problem, knowing the prevailing wind direction will help in placing shrubs and large trees to break the wind and make your yard more pleasant, plus help you save on heating costs in the winter.

Utilities and drain fields

"Call before you dig," the public-service announcements say, and they mean it. If you call 811 and tell them you're planning to relandscape your yard, you will be connected to your state's "one-call" center, and they will arrange to have a representative from each utility come out to your house and mark the underground lines. The marks will be in standard colors for each utility. Each one has a different minimum depth based on local codes, and you can find these out by calling your local agencies. Keep in mind, though, that not everything may have been installed to code; you might find a line shallower than you thought, so use extreme caution when digging where lines are marked.

If you have a septic system in your home, it would be a good idea to learn exactly where your drain field is. Drain fields cannot take any heavy machinery driving over them, and even foot traffic over them should be limited.

Neighbors, human and wild

Your naturescape design should take your neighbors into consideration. Do they introduce challenges that your design should address, such as a barking dog or kids who climb trees and look into your yard? Do they have concerns that you should take into consideration, such as solar panels that would be blocked by the tall windbreak trees you're thinking of planting? You might want to run your naturescaping ideas by them to see if they have any objections; most likely they will be happy that you are taking an interest in improving the appearance of your yard and the quality of your ecosystem, and they might get some ideas from you. In fact, you might just set off a naturescaping revolution in your neighborhood.

This observation period is also the time to notice animal visitors to your yard. Do the deer come down out of the hills at night to quietly graze in your garden? Do rabbits frequent the carrot patch? Do raccoons and possums forage for edibles in your compost pile? There are naturescaping solutions to equitably divide the harvest. Conversely, you may notice that your yard is bereft of animal and insect life, and you may see the need for a naturescape design that brings in birds, bees, and beneficial insects, as well as amphibians and small mammals.

Local laws, codes, and regulations

You'll need to find out if there are any local codes that might affect your naturescaping plans. The best place to start is your city hall or county offices. Finding information and getting permissions can be difficult and circuitous because the information you need might be in the Development, Environment, or Planning Department, or all three. You could ask to speak to the city landscape architect or city planner, or just start asking your question, such as "What are the fence height restrictions and setbacks for people on a corner lot?"

Check your local codes and regulations—they might limit how high your fences can be.

Regulations that might affect your naturescape design

❧ **Domestic animal regulations** limit the number of chickens, ducks, or rabbits you can keep. Many cities do not allow roosters within city limits.

❧ **Weed laws** specify how high grass can get. This is meant to keep down grass seed allergies, fire danger, and that vacant-lot look. You may have to fight these laws if you want to create a wildflower meadow (see the Wild Ones website at http://www.for-wild.org to find fellow combatants and cogent facts).

❧ **Fence height restrictions** limit the heights of fences along your property lines. Most cities do not allow fences within a certain "vision clearance area"—the corners of a property that may block a driver from seeing other cars, bikes, or pedestrians. Some cities allow only very low fences along the property line that runs parallel to the front door, which can be problematic for homeowners with corner properties.

❧ **Building setback requirements** prohibit buildings within a certain distance of your property lines, usually 10 feet.

❧ **Street tree restrictions** limit the types of trees that you can plant in your "hell strip" (that narrow planting bed between your sidewalk and curb) and, in some cases, in your front yard as well. Historically, cities have chosen a certain tree for a certain street, but that is changing as city deciders realize that a diverse "urban forest" is healthier. However, many cities do not allow certain trees for various reasons, or give you a limited list of trees from which to choose.

❧ **Fire hydrant regulations** specify no vegetation within a few feet of fire hydrants.

❧ **Neighborhood CC&R's** (covenants, conditions, and restrictions) can be more limiting that your city's municipal code. Some CC&R's do not allow for backyard chickens or hanging your laundry. Others allow only certain tree species. Check your house-purchase papers; if you are in a neighborhood with CC&R's, the contact information should be listed there.

Get Back to Nature

Once you have started a close study of the ecosystem of your own backyard, the next step in the naturescape design process is to get out into your region's larger ecosystem and see what design ideas you can pick up there. This is where naturescaping goes way beyond the simple advice to use only native plants in your garden. Further questions arise. Which natives? And what is a native? Native to this state? Pre-Columbian? Then there is the question of where in your yard these natives should go. Observing your region's ecological communities will give you the answers to these questions.

From ecoregion to backyard biohabitat

An ecological community is defined as all the organisms—not just plants and animals but also microorganisms—that live in a particular habitat and affect one another. Wherever you live, there is an ecological community nearby—and probably 5 or 10. California, for example, has 118 ecological communities, according to NatureServe, a nonprofit network of conservation data organizations. In the redwood forest ecosystem, some of the organisms working together are banana slugs, bobcats, mushrooms, moles, tanoaks, flies, wood strawberries, owls, beetles, woodpeckers, bats, columbine, black bears, sword ferns, wrens, poison oak, spotted owls, newts, lichen, salmon, hawks, California bay trees, eagles, and of course, those enormous redwoods.

The Northeast's oak-pine forest is another thriving ecosystem. Of course there are the oaks (white, chestnut, red, black, and scarlet) and the pines (white and pitch), but also sugar maples, beeches, birches, poplars, hickories, and chestnuts. Whip-poor-wills and cerulean warblers call through the forest canopy above the roaming moose and silent bobcat. At dusk, nighthawks and bats pursue their insect prey midair, diving and recovering, diving and recovering. Foraging under the laurels

The plants in this northeastern naturescape—yellowtwig dogwood, willow, winterberry, Virginia sweetspire, and northern bayberry—are typical of riparian communities in natural areas of the Northeast. Green Springs Gardens, Alexandria, VA.

and heaths, wild blueberries, and wintergreen are the white-footed mice, short-tailed shrew, hognose snake, and red-backed vole. Salamanders, newts, beetles, and spiders live, procreate, kill, and die among the mulch of fallen leaves. And below it all are the worms, fungi, bacteria, and undiscovered microbes breaking down the soil and feeding the towering trees.

These are large-scale ecosystems, but there is no reason that given the same climate and exposure, you could not borrow from what nature has created. For example, if you already have a grove of birches and sugar maples on your land, why not bring in the laurels and heaths, their usual companions? And leave the leaves, creating habitat for all the creepers and crawlers?

Once you become versed in the various ecological communities in your area, it will be easy to recognize similar situations in your own backyard—what I call backyard biohabitats. This will make it easier for you to select natives, or plants from another part of the country or world where ecological conditions are similar, that will thrive in your yard. A blending of natives and nonnative appropriates makes for a lovely and functional naturescape on many levels.

Take a hike!

The best way to learn about your region's ecological communities is to take a hike. Try to get out to every kind of ecosystem that your area has to offer. And if you find a brochure at the trailhead or visitor's center about what you are tromping though, be sure to take one; it probably has a list of the ecosystems you are in or the plants you are looking at. This knowledge will come in handy later when you are trying to remember which plants grow in which ecosystems that resemble parts of your own yard.

KNOW YOUR ECOSYSTEM WITH ONLINE HELP

To get a fix on ecological communities in your region, you can supplement your own observations in the outdoors with ecosystem descriptions available online. If you live in the United States, consult the ecosystems provinces pages on the U.S. Forest Service site at http://www.fs.fed.us/land/ecosys-mgmt/colorimagemap/ecoreg1_provinces.html. There you can click through from a map location to a description of the land-surface form, climate, vegetation, soils, and fauna of your ecoregion (ecosystem of regional extent). A McGill University project on Canada's ecozones offers a similar system at http://canadianbiodiversity.mcgill.ca/english/ecozones/ecozones.htm#map.

NATURAL AREAS TO EXPLORE IN YOUR COMMUNITY

federal wildlife refuges, national parks, and national forests

state preserves and state forests

county parks and open spaces

nature Conservancy preserves and private land trusts that allow pedestrian access

city natural areas for residents only

Visiting—and photographing—your local ecosystems is the best way to get familiar with native plant communities.

The national wildlife refuge that these eastern bluebirds frequent offers plentiful clues about habitats that would attract these birds to a backyard naturescape.

If you are hesitant to go on your own, find a group that sponsors hikes and join the next scheduled outing. Besides offering the obvious advantages of fresh air and camaraderie, group hikes are great because they are usually led by highly knowledgeable people who love to share what they know. On the other hand, these walks often end up being long on getting to know each other and short on getting to know your surroundings. So you could go on these scheduled hikes, enjoy the walk, then go again on your own or with another person who is very willing to go at a leisurely pace. Three-year-olds and people with canes are good for this.

GROUPS THAT SPONSOR HIKES

local nature and environmental centers

a "friends" chapter of a nearby national wildlife refuge (part of the U.S. Fish and Wildlife Service)

local soil and water conservation districts

local chapters of the National Audubon Society, Sierra Club, Izaak Walton League, and other national environmental groups

regional ecology groups such as the Surfrider Foundation, the Adirondack Mountain Club, and the Upper Chattahoochee River Keeper

community groups that sponsor special hikes as part of Earth Day celebrations

historical societies, historical trusts, city and regional agencies, and college campuses, which sponsor neighborhood walks that include tree identification, especially around Arbor Day (the last Friday in April) and historically significant days

And, if possible, get out there in all seasons. Some landscapes are completely transformed from one season to the next. As you experience these ecosystems, through the seasons and perhaps over the years, they will become a part of you and it will be much easier to create a landscape that reflects—and respects—these unique areas.

Develop the art of deep observation

If you get out there and stop often, you will start to notice things. You will notice which plants usually grow in association with which others, and under what conditions. You will learn how nature designs a forest edge or a meadow of wildflowers. You will note the layers of foliage in a forest or the way a particular plant is always seen with another particular plant.

Stopping by a creek, you might observe how quickly the water flows, how it forms ponds, what the rocks look like and whether they have variations in color, shape, or size. You'll observe how the rocks shape the flow of water (or is it the other way around?). Looking a little wider, you'll see how nearby foliage touches the water, and what the plants look like—woody? soft? spiky? slimy? If you are versed in plants, you might be able to identify them. Are they ferns, horsetails, marsh marigolds? Does the creek have dramatic waterfalls and grottos? Do the sides cut deeply into the land or is it a shallow depression? Does it meander or proceed in a relatively straight path? And finally, how does it sound?

I've found that taking photographs is a shortcut way of observing, so I don't rely on it as my only way of recording nature. I don't walk, shoot, walk walk walk. If I find an intriguing spot, I stay there for a while. I then take a few photos, mostly to remind myself of my experience, and move on. Later on, I use the photos to prompt my memories: "Ah, yes, I remember the way those two plants grew together on the bank of that creek." Some people draw, some take notes, some just sit. Whatever helps you to stay in that place and time, fully and completely, if only for a few minutes, is a good thing.

Deep observation is a bit of work, but it is profoundly satisfying. And it will make you a better designer, although you probably won't realize it until you are recreating a similar environment on your land. Say you decide to create a dry creek (rocks set in the ground to mimic a creek bed) in your front yard. Your memories, perhaps combined with your photos, will dictate how you cut into the soil, the stones you choose, and where you place each one. Then, when you step back and admire your work, you'll wonder how it turned out so natural looking.

Honor natural tendencies

Besides helping you identify backyard biohabitats and study nature's designs, getting out on hikes will help you be more aware of the climatic features and natural tendencies of your area. For example, if you live on a dry hillside in California, you should know that you are in wildfire country.

I live where it is almost always cloudy, with light precipitation going on. After nine months of this, we have a summer drought, many days with temperatures into the 90s, and fire danger. Therefore, it stands to reason that our planned landscapes should deal with the excessive winter rainwater, maximize winter sunlight, respect the summer drought, protect us from the hot summer sun, and be as fire resistant as possible. By contrast, a naturescaper in the Southwest might be dealing with flash floods, a caliche layer (bonded soil particles that create a barrier for roots), and, of course, extreme summer drought and heat.

Close observation of a creek can yield inspiration for a backyard water feature and knowledge about natural communities that populate wet areas. The Cary Institute for Ecosystem Studies.

This man-made seasonal streambed was inspired by close observation of a natural one
Design by Cynthia Rice.

So remember to look at the big picture, wherever you live. These natural occurrences and conditions are beyond our control, but ignoring them or trying to get around them just does not work. We end up with landscapes that need life support to survive. The horticulture industry and even garden writers like to play at the edges and push the envelope of common sense. Garden writers call it "zone denial" and have some fun with it; after all, it's a kick to see a tropical plant growing in Seattle. But it's no fun when those bright tropicals end up a gray mush-pile following a very cold night.

Now—early in the naturescape design process—is the time for you to think about these things. That's all you need to do for now. Later on, you will be challenged to create a naturescape that works within these conditions. No more pretending that "it" (deep snow, susceptibility to wildfire, or naturally parched land) is not there; a naturescape acknowledges and celebrates just what nature provides.

Explore Your Wants and Needs

While you're observing nature nearby as well as what's already in your yard, start asking yourself what you want from your naturescape. This is pie-in-the-sky time, when you can dream about how you're going to use your garden, the kinds of materials and plants you would like to incorporate, and what kind of theme or style you would prefer. You might want to make a copy of the questionnaire provided for you here and put it in your naturescaping binder, folder, or portfolio. Jot down your answers to the questions as you think about them over time.

You might also want to gather appealing images and ideas from magazines and books. Even though you may not be able to put your finger on what you like about the photos, or there are logistical—or just logical—reasons why you can't have a certain feature in your garden, it's a good exercise. What usually happens is that when all of the images are spread out on a table, a pattern may emerge that is more evocative than words. Couples or entire families can do this together, either by creating individual collages and presenting them to each other, or by having a "clipping party" that results in one big group collage. Either way, the result is a better understanding of each others' wants and needs, which makes for a better naturescape.

Have you always wanted an outdoor living room? This one features salvaged furniture, reused brick, and local stone.
Design by Jennifer Myers.

WORKSHEET 2: WHAT I WANT AND NEED

HOW YOU'RE GOING TO USE YOUR GARDEN

What is your vision for your property? Your front yard? Your backyard?

How do you see yourself (and other household members, if any) using your outdoor spaces on a typical day in summer? Fall? Winter? Spring?

Are there certain times of the year when you are especially interested in your garden? Certain times when you are not?

How many people do you expect to entertain outdoors? What types of gatherings will they be—informal, formal, family, business, community?

What are the elements that you would like to have in your yard (examples are a patio or sandbox)?

What areas of your property do you expect to be the most well used?

Do any people in your household have special needs or allergies that pertain to the landscaping? What about frequent guests and relatives?

If you have pets, do they have special requirements regarding landscaping?

Do you need a new or improved entrance to the front door?

Is your parking area adequate?

Do you need any more vehicle-tolerant surfaces than what you already have?

Are there areas where you want or need a footpath?

MATERIAL AND PLANT PREFERENCES

What kinds of materials do you envision using for surfaces and boundaries?

Are there certain plants that you really want in your garden for sentimental purposes, but that for other reasons you probably would not choose for your naturescape?

Are there any plants that you, or members of your family, just don't like?

STYLE PREFERENCES

Of the natural areas that you have visited, are there any that you still remember distinctly? What were they like and how did you feel?

Of the gardens you have visited, do you remember one that you really enjoyed? How would you describe it? How did it make you feel?

Are there any gardening magazines, websites, or books that you identify with?

When you think about various types of gardens throughout the world and throughout time, is there a certain one that you identify with? How would you describe it?

Are there any stylistic elements you would like to see in your garden, such as a decorative fountain, a Japanese deer scarer, a bean teepee, or a personal collection?

How you're going to use your garden

You may have a clear vision of what your natures-caped garden will look like. Most likely, though, you are so overwhelmed by your existing forlorn yard that you can't even imagine what it could be. An easy way to get out of that rut is to think about all the good times you can have, rather than what it will look like exactly. Badminton games and barbecue potlucks. Bird-watching, breakfast al fresco. Picking tomatoes and blueberries. Watching the grandkids ride their tricycles and climb trees. The idea here is to start imagining how, in your best life, you will enjoy your land.

With those good times in mind, you can then begin to assemble a wish list of landscape elements you might want or need. You can also begin to think about square footage, at least roughly, if you want a patio or decking. Will it be 150 square feet (the size of a 10 (15-foot room) or 375 square feet (a 15x25-foot room)? Get a feel for these sizes by measuring them out in your backyard. Then jot down the square footage you have in mind—not the dimensions—so you can be creative with shapes.

It's not too early to begin considering the details of the elements you want. For example, what kind of fire pit? What style of arbor? Start noticing—really noticing—the details when you look at gardens, gardening books, magazines, gardening TV shows, and even the backgrounds of movie scenes. Bring a camera when you go on a garden tour or visit a nice garden in your neighborhood (and don't be shy about asking to visit the back if you like the front). Inspiration, hate to say it, is rarely original. The good designer simply has good eyes and an open mind.

Chickens add fertilizer, food, and life to a naturescape.

ELEMENTS YOU MIGHT WANT
IN YOUR NATURESCAPE

FOOD AND FLOWERS

vegetable, herb, or cut-flower beds

orchard

FUN AND ENTERTAINMENT

patio or deck

seating

cooking area

arbor or gazebo

fire ring

swimming pool or pond

hot tub

special game area or outdoor court surface

children's play structure, playhouse, or tree house

CONSERVATION

rain garden, bioswale

water barrel, cistern

gray water wetland

green roof or green wall

compost bins or designated compost area(s)

nesting box or bat house

CONTEMPLATION

labyrinth

statues, prayer flags

yoga and/or meditation area

OUTBUILDINGS, STORAGE, UTILITY

shelter for chickens, ducks, and/or rabbits

studio, guest room, or pool house

greenhouse

potting bench or shed

toy or equipment storage

tool storage

recycling cart or bins

trash storage

FENCING AND WALLS

new fences or a freestanding wall

retaining wall

CIRCULATION AND PARKING

path to the front door

path encircling the house

off-street parking

Material and plant preferences

The built elements of your garden such as patios and walkways, sometimes called the hardscape, can be made from any number of materials—for instance, brick, flagstone, gravel, concrete, or asphalt. The material you choose for each hardscape element gives it a certain character. If it helps you to visualize a particular element, by all means think about the material you might want to employ, but it is not crucial to the design as of now—and in fact it might limit your thought process. So, for now, think "patio" and be open to the many possibilities that your mind can explore. Later you will learn some environmental reasons why some materials are more desirable than others in a naturescape.

Similarly, now is the time to think about but not decide on the kinds of plants you would like in your naturescape. Jot down old sentimental favorites; if they aren't appropriate to the conditions your site provides, you may be able to identify native or appropriate replacements when it comes time to make plant choices. Conversely, there might be plants that you are allergic to or plants you just don't like. Note these plants on your questionnaire.

Style preferences

A naturescape does not need to look like nearby nature, though it might. After spending time in local natural areas, you may decide that you would like a garden with a naturalistic style. Or you may have noticed in visiting local gardens that you feel drawn to create an English cottage garden, an Italian villa, or a Japanese garden. A Northwest casual style (meandering walks, natural materials), a Southwest style (bright and earthy hues, unfinished wood, rugged stone pavers), or a contemporary style (straight lines and masses of the same plant within each bed) may appeal to you. Any of these styles can be incorporated in a naturescape.

A naturescape respects, learns from, and copies nearby natural processes but can be of any style we choose. Even a formal garden can be built with naturescaping concepts. For example, a formal garden will most likely have straight or uniformly curved paths. Naturescaping encourages use of local materials that would otherwise go to waste, so a naturescaped formal garden might have straight paths made of crushed oyster shells from a local cannery or hazelnut husks from a nearby orchard. In the geometrically shaped beds, why not plant natives? And formal terraces? They go with the naturescaping concept of maximizing rainwater infiltration.

Similarly, a fan of the Japanese garden might incorporate fencing with bamboo harvested from a friend's yard, a handmade deer scarer, and a large water bowl next to the front door. These are not out of the realm of naturescaping. As long as the gardener doesn't rake away the fallen leaves from the beds underneath her beautiful Japanese maples, it's still a naturescape.

CHAPTER 1 HOMEWORK:
GET TO KNOW YOUR PLACE ON EARTH

- ☐ *Start a naturescaping binder, folder, or portfolio.*
- ☐ *Observe your land and complete worksheet 1, "What I Already Have."*
- ☐ *Photograph your yard.*
- ☐ *Learn about your region's ecological communities by taking hikes and doing Internet research.*
- ☐ *Complete worksheet 2, "What I Want and Need."*
- ☐ *Gather appealing images.*

Although this Connecticut garden is formal in style, it is a naturescape in fact. The lawn and perennials were chosen to survive without the need for synthetic fertilizers or supplemental watering. The lawn is a permeable walking surface that, unlike concrete or quarried stone, did not use up fossil fuels in its creation (although it does need occasional mowing). Design by Joan Larned.

chapter two

GO WITH THE FLOW

Manage runoff and reduce your need for supplementary water to protect local waterways and water supplies.

You've begun the naturescape design process with close observation of your piece of the earth. The next step is to begin thinking through the wider ecological implications of any design decisions you make. Considering your use and handling of water is a key piece of that understanding.

Looking at your land as part of a larger ecosystem—a watershed—will help you see why it's important to give some thought to reducing your water runoff. Also essential is the realization that clean water is a precious and increasingly expensive resource. Even in areas that normally experience year-round abundance, periodic droughts are possible—particularly as climate patterns change and a growing population puts increasing pressure on the supply. This means you need to make water awareness a part of your naturescape design.

Keep Your Water on Your Land

Rain gutters, downspouts, and storm drains are so much a part of the urban and suburban landscape that we don't give them a second thought. But from a naturescaping point of view, these fixtures of modern life could use rethinking because they have a cumulative negative impact on the health of our waterways. Let's look at the reasons to keep your water on your land and some strategies you might use to do so.

Runoff: Bad news for rivers

Houses are made to keep the rain out, and driveways are made so our heavy cars won't get stuck in the mud when the rains come. So what do we do with the water that falls on rooftops and driveways? The conventional thinking goes: sheet it off and pipe it to the nearest waterway. It sounds reasonable; a few streets, a few houses, a few driveways draining to a nearby creek is like pouring an extra cupful of water into a filled (but draining) bathtub. But picture putting that cup on your kitchen floor and filling it with the bathtub water. In most cities (and their surrounding suburbs), the creek is the cup and the piped water during a storm is the full bathtub.

When the flow of piped water is fast and furious, streams "incise" (become unnaturally deep with unwalkably steep banks), and the eroded sediments cloud the water, which prevents aquatic organisms from finding food and habitat. That piped storm water, fresh off pavement and rooftops, is relatively warm. Water that's warmer by just a few degrees can damage—even ruin—some stream ecosystems. When streams suffer, the insects and animals that depend on these streams suffer too. Fish are especially sensitive to changes in temperature, and populations become diseased. In the Pacific Northwest, for example, storm water runoff is considered one of the major causes of the dramatic decline and near extinction of salmon. Delicate pollination and predator systems, even miles away from the stream, can be damaged or even ruined as well.

Storm water is laden with sediments: air pollutants that settle on our roofs, tire and brake dust and oils from roadways, and pet waste and chemical contaminants from our yards. This is what ecologists call nonpoint-source pollution—pollution that doesn't originate from a single source (like a factory) but comes from everywhere in the environment and has a big cumulative effect. This kind of pollution includes excess pesticides and fertilizers applied to lawns and gardens. Studies have found that the average suburban lawn is drenched with ten times as much chemical pesticide per acre as farmland. Because a lawn has less than 10 percent of the water absorption capacity of a natural woodland, chemicals applied to lawns are particularly prone to runoff and leaching.

No wonder the city of Portland, Oregon, and its soil and water conservation district has increasingly promoted the idea, borrowed from the Oregon Department of Fish and Wildlife, of "naturescaping for clean rivers." Other organizations and government agencies around the country are catching on to this idea as well. There may be a program in your area that educates homeowners about watershed issues connected to backyard stewardship.

When more gardeners adopt the old-fashioned ethic of "waste not, want not," it will go a long way toward decreasing nonpoint-source pollution of our waterways. If you're like most homeowners, you pay for clean water to be piped into your home, and you use some of this expensive commodity to water your landscape. At the same time, you pay for rainwater to be piped away from your property. Check your water bill—usually it will include a "storm water system surcharge" or some such item. In essence, you're paying to have free water taken away. It's the modern way, but a few generations ago people were smarter. Rain barrels, holding tanks, cisterns, and wells were common in our great-grandparents' day.

KNOW YOUR WATERSHED

"We all live in a watershed—the area that drains to a common waterway, such as a stream, lake, estuary, wetland, aquifer, or even the ocean—and our individual actions can directly affect it," admonishes the U.S. Environmental Protection Agency (EPA). You can locate your own watershed and learn more about local citizen-based groups by visiting the EPA's "Surf Your Watershed" website (http://www.epa.gov; enter "surf your watershed" in the search box). Your local soil and water conservation district is also a rich source of information regarding your watershed and issues connected to it. (Technically, a watershed is the ridge that separates one drainage basin from another. In the United States and Canada, however, the term usually refers to the drainage basin itself.)

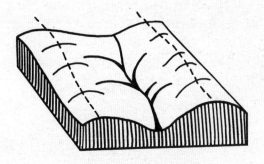

A watershed is the area that drains to a common waterway.

By piping rainwater away from your land you lose more than just water. When rainwater soaks into the earth, microorganisms in soil break down associated sediments and pollutants, resulting in plant-available nitrogen, phosphorus, potassium, and calcium: nutrients your plants thrive on. That's another good reason not to let your storm water run away but instead to use it for irrigating your landscape. Following are some ideas on how you might do this.

Disconnect your downspouts

The most obvious way to keep your rainwater is to disconnect your downspouts and route the water onto your land one way or another. Check with your local zoning or building authorities first to see if this is legal, and if so, if it requires permits where you live. Then find out whether your particular drainage situation makes your yard a good candidate for disconnection; having steep slopes or poorly draining soils will mean it's not such a good candidate. You should also find out where your downspouts currently discharge to help you think about what to do with the water. You might discover that your neighbors could be affected; if so, get them on board with any water retention system you consider.

You have a number of options for routing your downspout water. If you have enough room, the ground slopes away from your house, and water percolates into your soil reasonably quickly, you can simply extend your downspout and discharge the water onto your lawn or into an adjacent planting bed. This is what most people do. You can choose to direct the water to a small pond, or to a bioswale or rain garden. You may opt to install a cistern or rain barrel, a clever way to save it for a sunny day.

Bioswales and rain gardens direct and retain runoff while also broadening your planting options. They consist of a shallow dip (generally not more than a foot deep so that water won't pool) vegetated with native water-loving plants that either routes runoff somewhere (in which case it's called a bioswale) or holds it for long enough to soak into the ground (in which case it's called a rain garden). A rain garden allows about 30 percent more water to soak into the ground than a lawn would. These water-retaining features should be located at least 6 feet from your house's foundation, 10 feet if you have a basement. You also might think about planting a rain garden if there's an area of your yard that has seasonal standing water. (Don't have downspout runoff go here, though.)

Ponds are another option for retaining stormwater. You can dig a pond into clay soil, or install a rubber liner if you have sandy soil (avoiding a PVC liner as PVC is damaging to the environment in its manufacture, and most municipalities do not accept it for recycling). A pond should be located downhill from the house and at least 10 feet from the foundation. Rain barrels or cisterns are a great way to capture and reuse rainwater where there are short periods of drought, such as in the Midwest, the Northeast, or the Southeast.

Rain barrels are generally available at lawn and garden stores most of the year and are relatively simple to install. Some cities, such as Olympia, Washington, offer rebates to homeowners who install them. Keep in mind, though, that a single 55-gallon rain barrel fills pretty quickly during a rainstorm and may not make much of a dent in your water needs during an extended dry period in the summer. Cisterns, available at farm supply stores, are larger tanks that can be aboveground or underground and may work better for homeowners with larger lots.

LAWS REGARDING DOWNSPOUT DISCONNECTION

It might be illegal or require special permits and permissions to change your storm water system, based on laws meant to prevent standing water, property damage, and spread of waterborne disease. But things are changing. Forward-thinking municipalities are realizing that systems of storm water management are possible that don't harm the environment yet still protect against flooded basements and malaria outbreaks. They're even encouraging homeowners to try these alternatives. If your town or county doesn't yet allow such alternatives, perhaps it's time to have a meeting with your city councillor or county commissioner. A little Internet research will turn up lots of studies that you can use to convince them that a more relaxed approach toward rainwater is in their best interest.

A swimming pond, or a natural swimming pool that uses no chlorine, can be augmented with rainwater. This natural swimming pool uses peripheral "regeneration areas" filled with aquatic plants to keep it clean. When it rains, water drains directly into the pool from its rock-lined rim.

This home in the Northwest reduces storm water runoff in two ways: a roof garden soaks up most of the rainwater and any excess is routed to the rain garden below. The rush planted in the foreground on the right is great for western rain gardens because it can handle drought as well as flooding. Design by Habitats, Inc.

HOW TO DISCONNECT A DOWNSPOUT

To disconnect a downspout from its underground connection is usually a simple procedure that you can accomplish in less than an hour with a hacksaw, a drill, and a screwdriver, plus a cap for your sewer standpipe and an elbow to attach an extension to the downspout. Saw through the downspout or unhook it from its connection, cap the connection, attach an elbow to the downspout, and then attach an extension to the elbow.

A simple downspout extension is relatively cheap and easy to install and generally performs well. You can route it to a splash block or bury it underground up to the point where you want it to discharge water. Because metal extensions eventually rust through if they're buried, use plumbing-grade ABS pipe for a buried extension. You can also route a downspout extension under a walkway or have it discharge through buried perforated pipe over a distance. Or get creative and use the water to set ornamental items in motion or drain out of statues. Rain chains are just the start of the endless possibilities for using the flow of water through your garden.

Keep in mind that you don't need to disconnect all of your downspouts; you can disconnect just one if that's all the runoff you have the capacity to handle in your yard. Also, you can install a downspout diverter that can be turned on and off to fill a rain barrel or cistern. When the container is full, this handy device lets you direct the water back into the downspout.

PROTECT YOUR PROPERTY FROM WATER DAMAGE

Regardless of how you handle water from a disconnected downspout, keep in mind these guidelines from the Office of Planning and Development Review for the city of Portland, Oregon:

• If you disconnect to a surface system (including splash blocks, swales, or ponds) the land adjacent to your house must slope away from the house so that surface water doesn't pond or soak into the ground close to the foundation.

• Your disconnected downspouts must discharge away from the edge of your house. For houses with basements, downspout extensions should discharge at least 6 feet from the house. For houses without basements, downspout extensions should discharge at least 2 feet from the house.

• Avoid directing downspout water into an area that is too small for good drainage or too close to a retaining wall.

• Your downspouts should discharge at least 5 feet from your neighbor's property line and you should not disconnect downspouts where the side of your house is less than 10 feet from an adjacent neighbor's house. If your house is higher than your neighbor's property, the appropriate protective distance may be greater.

• For any surface system you intend to install, you should visualize where the slope of your yard will direct runoff under the wettest conditions. In all cases, flow from downspout extensions or overflow from a drainage swale or pond should not create a drainage problem for your neighbors.

BUILD A SIMPLE RAIN GARDEN

If you want to build your own rain garden, start by considering what you've learned by observing your land. The ideal spot is one that water naturally flows to during heavy rainfalls but where it does not stand for long before percolating into the soil. (If your soil percolates at less than ½ inch per hour, you should not create a rain garden.) Also, your rain garden should be located where an emergency outflow pipe can connect to the traditional drainage method such as a street gutter or storm drain. Do not build a rain garden over your septic system or within 10 feet of your house's foundation.

The second step is to determine how large your rain garden should be to handle the water that will be flowing into it. A rain garden in sandy soil should cover 20 percent of the area draining to it; in loamy soil, 20 to 60 percent; in clay soil, 60 percent. Figure out the square footage of the surface area that will drain into your rain garden. For example, if a downspout draining into your garden channels the runoff from a roof measuring 15 by 20 feet, this will be 300 square feet. Then multiply that by the recommended percentage to get the square footage of your rain garden; in the case of clay soil, this will be 180 square feet.

Your rain garden can be 6 to 24 inches deep; the better the percolation of your soil, the shallower the rain garden can be. Rain gardens usually have curvy edges and are level at the bottom with sloping sides. Use the soil you excavate from the garden to build a berm on the downhill side in order to help keep the water in the garden. Cover this, as well as the upper edge of the rain garden, with grass or ground cover to hold the soil.

Surprisingly, not all of the plants you choose for your rain garden should be wetland plants. The ones at the bottom of the slope, yes, but the plants along the sides might need to tolerate extensive periods of drought. Sedges and rushes are ideal. Mulch with 3 inches of a dense material like pine straw, wood chips, or gravel. For more details, including a list of plants suitable for rain gardens, see the Clean Water Campaign's brochure on rain gardens at http://www.epa.gov/owow_keep/NPS/toolbox/other/cwc_raingardenbrochure.pdf.

If local regulations permit, you can disconnect your downspout and allow your rooftop rainwater to seep into the soil. Hostas and astilbes thrive in the near-constant moisture that the downspout in this Northwest garden provides nine months out of the year.

This permeable driveway adds interest to the yard while allowing rainwater and car drips to be cleansed by the soil below. Design by Dawn Jones.

Permeable paving is nothing new, as this 700-year-old street in Tuscany, Italy, illustrates. It drains well in the rain, the weeds stay down with traffic (pedestrians, carts, motorbikes, and cars), and water flows into the soil.

Make surfaces permeable

Another approach to retaining water on your land is to make previously impervious surfaces—concrete paths, asphalt driveways, tarps, black plastic—permeable. Impervious surfaces repel water, sometimes sending it into the storm water system. It's the surfaces in your yard that drain into your city storm water system that we're concerned with here, which I emphasize because sometimes people forget that the reason for using permeable surfaces in the landscape is to avoid sending runoff into storm drains. If the water drains from an impervious surface into adjacent soil, no problem. Keep that in mind when you're deciding if your brick path should be set in concrete or sand. Either way, it'll drain into the adjacent planting beds, so if your soil infiltration rate is reasonable, from a runoff standpoint it just doesn't matter.

Most often, your driveway is your main culprit—and maybe your sidewalk. Driveways account for a lot of pollution entering our waterways. Whatever shows up on your driveway eventually ends up in your nearest creek, river, or ocean: car drippings, phosphorus from washing your car, fertilizer granules, or pesticides. One way to limit harmful driveway runoff is to be more conscientious—keep your car in the garage (with cardboard underneath that you eventually compost), wash your car on your lawn, and don't use synthetic fertilizers or pesticides.

Another way is to make your driveway permeable. Check first with your local municipality to see if this requires a permit or permission. You can lift your existing concrete driveway, break it up into smaller pieces, and re-lay them upside down for a pretty mosaic effect. Or you may opt for a gravel driveway. How about bringing back the old-fashioned 1-foot-wide strip of grass down the middle of the driveway (to soak up grease and oil)? Or perhaps you'll replace your concrete driveway with interconnected concrete blocks that let the water pass through, or with turfblock, concrete blocks with openings in a honeycomb

pattern where grass grows. Other options include gravel, porous concrete, or porous asphalt. (Remember that replacing your concrete driveway is an ecological choice only if you recycle or reuse the old concrete.)

Porous concrete (also known as permeable concrete, no-fines concrete, gap-graded concrete, and enhanced-porosity concrete) is something you might want to look into if you're creating a new driveway or patio. Because of its combination of strength and rainwater permeability, the EPA recommends it as one of its "best management practices," and savvy municipalities are requiring it for new parking lots. Water flows through it because 15 to 25 percent of the material is "voids" created by omitting sand from the mix. Carefully controlled amounts of water and cementitious materials create a paste that when cured has the strength to support a large, loaded vehicle.

Pervious asphalt follows the same principle of creating voids within the mix, by omitting the smaller particles and reducing the tar percentage. This technology has been around since the 1970s. Perhaps the best known application is the parking lot at Walden Pond; since the lot is within 300 feet of the pond—a popular destination for swimmers, picnickers, hikers, rowers, cross-country skiers, and snowshoers—the Massachusetts Department of Conservation and Recreation repaved the lot in 1977 to eliminate runoff and guard the health of the water.

If you live in a large metropolitan area, you can find a contractor that offers these options—or even specializes in them—and they will cost no more than traditional methods. However, in a smaller community you might get a puzzled look when suggesting pervious concrete or asphalt to a contractor—and higher bids, even double the bid price for traditional methods. That's not fleecing; it's just that the contractor needs to factor in the learning curve for your climatic conditions and the higher potential for errors and re-dos.

There are drawbacks to pervious concrete or asphalt, however. One is that if the infiltration rate of your native soil is poor, you may need to bring in soil amendments before laying the new concrete or asphalt; you will need a professional contractor to do this. Another is that you will need to have someone remove sediments and leaves every few months with a parking-lot vacuum or vacuum-sweeper, or rent one yourself.

Finally, you can make your soil surface more permeable by increasing the amount of organic matter—compost and mulch; really anything that was once alive—in your soil, because this material acts like a big sponge. Adding organic matter is the key to remedying much of what ails the world, and healing your local waterways is just one instance. You'll read more about the importance of healthy soil and how to keep it that way later in the book, but for now just note that healthy soil helps reduce runoff.

Green your roof

Our prairie forebears living in sod houses were green-roof pioneers; think *Little House on the Prairie* by Laura Ingalls Wilder. A green roof is a layer of vegetation installed on top of a building, like the layer of sod on top of sod houses. Modern green roofs are generally equipped with a water-proof membrane, a soil substrate, and living plants. The idea is to reduce (or eliminate) rooftop runoff. Green roofs are particularly well suited to situations where there's no land nearby for the roof to drain to, such as in a city or downtown, but they're also a decorative and functional option for topping garden sheds, balconies, garage roofs, and homes in other settings. They have the added advantages of keeping the building below warmer in the winter and cooler in the summer, insulating against sound, attracting wildlife, and offering planting space that can support a surprisingly wide range of plants.

A green roof needs to be designed and installed with great care. As of this writing, there is no national certification system for either designers or installers, so for now you are on your own (although movements are being made). A licensed landscape architect would be your best bet for a safe and workable design, and an experienced landscape contractor who could work with an experienced roofer would also be the way to go.

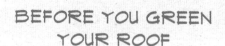

BEFORE YOU GREEN YOUR ROOF

- Check to see if local building codes allow green roofs.

- Determine whether your roof has an acceptable pitch: between 1:12 (5 degrees) and 5:12 (20 degrees). You can eyeball it from the ground or go up and measure.

- Find out if your roof is or can be made completely waterproof.

- Figure out whether your roof can bear the weight. A growing medium that's between 3 and 4 inches deep can weigh somewhere between 205 and 225 pounds per square foot. Professional advice from an architect or structural engineer may be needed here.

- Recognize that you may need to water your green roof periodically to keep it alive, depending on your climate, and think about how you're going to do this. You may want to install a drip system.

A green roof soaks up rainwater like a sponge, keeping our waterways clean. This roof also provides seeds for wildlife and helps the building blend in with the landscape.

Arbors and vines can cool a garden and reduce its need for water. This arbor was made with reclaimed porch brackets and wood once used in bookshelves. Design by Resourceful Judith Designs.

Be Water Wise

Very few, if any, of us live in a climate that gives us just the right amount of water at every time of year. More likely, our cup runneth over during some months and goes bone dry during others. Winter excess may be counterbalanced by summer drought. Water wisdom is learning what nature gives your property in the way of rainfall—when, how, and where—and what you can do to maximize (or minimize) it for the overall health of your landscape. We've looked at ways to minimize the water that runs off your land during periods of excess moisture. Now we turn to considering how to make the wisest use of whatever moisture is present during the driest periods.

What's wrong with piping water to plants that need more than just what falls from the sky during the driest months of the year? After all, in communities across the United States, irrigation is mandated in building codes. We want our neighborhoods to look lush and green when it's hot outside, don't we?

The problem is that in those places where nature doesn't offer summer rain, the water has to come from somewhere else. In the West, where the dry season coincides with the growing season, a rapidly increasing population is sucking rivers dry to keep unnatural expanses of lawn and other water wasters on life support. The fish and other critters that call those rivers home are going belly up. This is the very definition of unsustainability. As water becomes scarcer, its price goes up, and along with it the cost of maintaining a water-wasting landscape.

For the health of your pocketbook as well as of those other species that need water to survive, think about minimizing your use of summer water as you plan your naturescape. Regardless of where you live, a zero-irrigation goal for ornamental landscapes is both achievable (with some exceptions) and unquestionably laudable. Some ways you can approach this include limiting your lawn area, xeriscaping with drought-tolerant plants, and considering carefully how to irrigate if you absolutely need to.

DESIGN FOR LOW WATER USAGE

- Place deciduous trees south and west of your home. The plants beneath will be shaded in the summer, thus needing less water, but the winter sun will come into your home when you most need it.

- Site potentially heat-reflecting walls and pathways away from the harsh afternoon sun.

- Layer plant materials vertically to shade and cool the soil below.

- Add arbors and trellises and cover them with vines to moderate the sun.

- Terrace hillsides to increase the area of land you can plant, conserve moisture, and prevent erosion.

Terracing is a great way to retain water on a hillside, reducing runoff and thus keeping waterways clean. This hillside is terraced with local stone and planted with drought-tolerant plants such as brown-eyed Susan and lamb's ears.
Design by Karen Bussolini.

Limit your lawn

We plant overly large lawns for reasons buried in the past and our own psyches—lawns mean picnics and barbecues, birthday parties and throwing the ball around with Dad—and perhaps under the mistaken impression that maintaining a lawn is easier and cheaper than maintaining a more varied landscape. But if we live in a climate with arid summers, we end up pouring water on our lawns to keep them alive. According to the nonprofit organization PlantNative, 60 percent of water consumed in the western United States goes to lawns; in the East, it's 30 percent. And the accompanying mowers and blowers contribute noise and air pollution that we really don't need.

Lawns do have their place. Lush lawns are components of some of the most beautiful gardens in North America, from Monticello to Filoli. They are a perfect contrast to the variety of shapes, colors, and textures in the garden, unifying all with a simple sward of green. In the front yard, a strip of lawn next to the sidewalk creates a nice visual transition from the horizontal street to the upright perennials and shrubs, softening the verticality of the house.

But consider how much lawn you really need. A good rule of thumb is to plant or keep only as much as you can mow with a push mower, which is a great way to get exercise and talk to passers-by. With less lawn come larger planting beds, which allow more room for a variety of heights, foliage colors and textures, and flowers. What's more, this allows for larger plants, plants that relate well to the scale of the outdoors and add depth to the scene, which can be visually satisfying.

A small lawn is much better for the environment—and easier on you—than a vast expanse of green. This small patch of drought-tolerant buffalo grass needs no mowing.

Even if you do have some lawn, you don't have to keep it irrigated if you live in an area where grass naturally goes dormant in the summer. If you don't water your grass in the dry season, it won't die (presuming it's a perennial grass). It will spring back to life with the first rains. If your neighbor has a problem with that, make a lawn sign that says, "This lawn isn't dead, it's just sleeping," like the one the City of Olympia, Washington, distributes to its residents.

You should also be aware that there are less thirsty alternatives to the traditional lawn-seed mixes. For example, buffalo grass, *Buchloe dactyloides*—a shortgrass native to the high plains of the West, the Midwest, and the Southwest—is drought, heat, and cold resistant, and it spreads aggressively to make a dense turf that needs little or no mowing. And then there are the "ecology" lawn mixes, which blend grasses, clovers, wildflowers, and herbs. Lawns from these mixes need 50 to 75 percent less water than traditional grass lawns, and less mowing as well, and they demand no fertilizers or pesticides. National distributors of these mixes are Nichols Garden Nursery in Albany, Oregon (http://www.nicholsgardennursery.com), and Hobbs and Hopkins in Portland, Oregon (http://www.protimelawnseed.com).

You might also try low-growing meadow and prairie grasses that grow naturally in your region. Using low-growing herbs and other perennials that can function as lawn substitutes makes particular sense in the summer-drought regions of the Southwest and West. For very large expanses, you might consider a meadow garden. *The American Meadow Garden: Creating a Natural Alternative to the Traditional Lawn* by John Greenlee offers ideas and information.

Xeriscape

Xeriscaping is landscaping with plants, usually native but not necessarily, that look lovely yet don't suck up the water. And as it turns out, plants that require less water usually also require less maintenance (if grown in the right backyard biohabitat). In general, drought-tolerant plants prefer well-draining soil and do need a touch of supplemental water, an inch every two weeks or so, during the hottest part of peak growing season. A word of caution: a few drought-tolerant plants may be regarded as outlaws in some areas, usually because they are so low-care that they proliferate to the point of annoyance or fire danger. Look for online and print sources of information on drought-tolerant plants appropriate to your neck of the woods.

LOW-WATER LAWN SUBSTITUTES

Achillea millefolium (common yarrow)

Dymondia margaretae (silver carpet)

Festuca ovina glauca (blue fescue)

Juniperus procumbens (decumbent juniper)

Sedum species (stonecrop)

Thymus pseudolanuginosus (woolly thyme)

Thymus serpyllum (creeping thyme)

Trifolium repens (white clover)

"Eco Lawn"

Developed by Tom Cook, Associate Professor Emeritus of Horticulture, the Weatherford lawn is designed to be an enviromentally friendlier lawn requiring reduced mowing, irrigation, fertilizer and pesticides, while providing a lawn enjoyable for conventional use. The "Eco Lawn" consists of Perennial Ryegrass, Strawberry Clover, Yarrow, and Daisies

An ecology lawn such as this one on the Oregon State University campus needs 50 to 75 percent less water than traditional lawns and requires no fertilizers or pesticides.

Irrigate intelligently

You may have a preference for plants that aren't drought-tolerant; that's your prerogative. However, you can still choose to irrigate in an ecologically responsible manner. Hand watering, drip irrigation, and soaker hoses are such methods. And if you want to design a system that doesn't use city or well water, you can use gray water. Whichever method you choose, putting a layer of compost or other mulch at least 3 inches deep on top of your beds is essential in order to keep moisture in the soil (and also keep weeds down).

My favorite way to conserve water is to hand water. Because I am watering each plant based on its individual need, no water is wasted. And it gets me out there every few days, no matter how busy I am, since I can't let my plants die! Then I see the new blossoms and smell the soil—and wonder why I didn't get out there sooner. Every time I give my garden a drink, I get so much more in return.

Drip irrigation, in which water drips from emitters placed next to each plant, wastes less water than traditional spray irrigation systems. Be aware, though, that it takes money and time to install a drip irrigation system. Also, because watering this way is automatic, it removes you a bit from your garden's water needs. And it might be used as an excuse for planting thirsty exotics. Another nonspray solution is to place soaker hoses (in which water slowly "sweats" out of a hose) in your beds, but these have the disadvantage of watering the bare spots between plants, which is wasteful and can encourage weed growth.

XERISCAPING FAVORITES

TREES

Calocedrus decurrens (incense cedar)

Eucalyptus species

Ficus carica (edible fig)

Quercus species (oak)

SHRUBS, SUBSHRUBS, AND VINES

Lavandula species (lavender)

Punica granatum (pomegranate)

Ribes species (currant)

Rosmarinus species (rosemary)

Vitis vinifera (grape)

Yucca species

PERENNIALS AND ANNUALS

Echinacea species (coneflower)

Hemerocallis species (daylily)

Rudbeckia species (black-eyed Susan)

Salvia species (sage)

Sedum species (stonecrop)

Tropaeolum majus (nasturtium)

A "no-mow" lawn is a mix of naturally short grasses that can be walked—or played—on, giving the yard a meadowy feel. Designed by Shades of Green Landscape Architecture.

A xeriscape can look just as lush and colorful as any tropical garden. This yard in Austin, Texas, has been planted with low-water plants, including sunrose, rosemary, and buffalo grass.

Too much water from overhead spraying is lost to evaporation or ends up on a plant's foliage, where it isn't needed. A drip system waters the root zone, which is much more efficient.

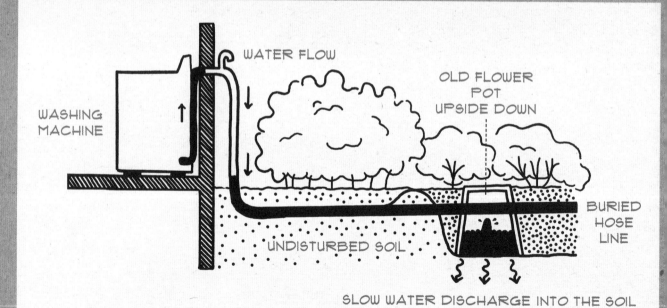

WATER FLOW

OLD FLOWER
POT
UPSIDE DOWN

WASHING
MACHINE

BURIED
HOSE
LINE

UNDISTURBED SOIL

SLOW WATER DISCHARGE INTO THE SOIL

Your household's gray water can be used to water your plants, if your state allows it. This sketch illustrates how a gray water system might work: soapy water from a washing machine is piped outside to a hose that passes through undisturbed soil into a basin where some of the water is let out to percolate into the soil. An upside-down nursery pot keeps the hose in place and protects it from errant shovels.

And then there is gray water: the water that drains out of your bathtub, sinks, dishwasher, and washing machine. This water is actually pretty good for plants, and you can rig up a system to get it to them. Your municipality or state may not allow using gray water for landscape purposes, however, so check with your local authorities. But things are changing, and sometimes when common sense meets "but we've always done it this way," common sense wins. Such is the case in California, where gray water usage for landscape purposes has been legal since 1989. There gray water systems are designed with health and safety in mind, allowing it to be disbursed in the landscape only through underground drip irrigation lines of a specific depth and quality.

If you want to create a gray water system and it's illegal where you live, there's probably a group of like-minded people who are lobbying for change; join them. If you want to create a gray water system and it's legal where you live, your municipality probably has regulations and inspection fees, so be sure to contact the appropriate authority. They can also direct you to licensed plumbers who can set up such a system for you. A wealth of information on every aspect of gray water systems can be found on the Oasis Design website at http://oasisdesign.net/grey-water/index.htm.

CHAPTER 2 HOMEWORK:
MANAGE RUNOFF AND REDUCE YOUR NEED FOR SUPPLEMENTARY WATER

- ☐ Observe how water passes through your land and learn about your local watershed.

- ☐ Consider disconnecting your downspouts and adding a bioswale or rain garden.

- ☐ Investigate making your driveway permeable.

- ☐ Look into reducing runoff with a green roof.

- ☐ Plan to reduce (or eliminate) your lawn and/or refrain from watering when your lawn is naturally dormant.

- ☐ Start learning about drought-tolerant plants that thrive in your area.

- ☐ Instead of a spray irrigation system, think about hand watering, drip emitters, or soaker hoses.

- ☐ Consider reusing your household water by installing a gray water system (or advocating the legalization, in your state, of reusing household water).

chapter three

MATCH PLANT
TO PLACE

Put the right plant in the right place, based on function, needs, and natural communities.

Plants define the garden. In a naturescape, we choose plants with knowledge of not only what they can do for us and what they need but also what our land can naturally provide, and we group them in communities that might be found in nature. It may seem inside-out from the usual (populate the garden with plants from anywhere in the world as long as they can withstand the winter, then spend lots of energy and money keeping these fussy out-of-towners happy) and it may require more work in the short term, but a well-planned naturescape demands less and less from us as it matures into a functioning ecosystem.

This approach is not so new, but it has been slow to catch on. In 1984, the publication of *Right Plant, Right Place* by Nicola Ferguson signaled a distinct departure from what gardeners of the 1950s through 1970s had been taught, mostly by articles and advertisements touting the wide range of exotics that could be kept alive on life support (water, fertilizer, pesticides) in the suburban yard. Instead, this innovative book grouped plants according to their preferred growing conditions (such as clay soil, deep shade, or seasonal flooding) and showed gardeners an alternative to spraying, clipping, mowing, raking, fertilizing, and watering the yard just to keep it all alive. "Right plant, right place" became a classic gardening adage.

But you may still be working too hard to keep inappropriate plants alive and healthy looking. In this chapter you will take the next step in designing your naturescape, which is to focus on learning about plants and choosing the right ones for your yard based on its biohabitats. You will inventory the plants you already have and decide if any need to be moved or removed. You will scope out your soil. Then you will map your backyard biohabitats to help you identify the easy-to-grow plants for your yard. You will start your plant list, paying attention to including a healthy diversity of various kinds of plants.

Take your time with this step, go online and research botanical names, go to nurseries and botanical gardens and websites, and learn all you can about the plants best suited to your site. And please note that some plants considered invasive or noxious in one region are terrific garden picks for other regions. Choose and plant knowingly and responsibly for your region.

Inventory the Plants Already in Your Yard

Now is the time to take stock of your existing plants. You will need to determine what stays, what is to be moved, and what is to be removed. You will also want to find out if there are any rare or endangered plants on your property, or any noxious weeds.

To get started, walk around your property with two colors of landscape tape (brightly-colored 1/2-inch-wide plastic tape, available at hardware stores) and tie short lengths to the branches of plants to signal "move" or "remove." I use blue for "move" and red for "remove." If it stays, or you are not sure yet, it receives no tape. This might feel a little like putting the cart ahead of the horse; how do you know if you will want to remove something? Keep in mind that this is a first pass; tag the obvious ones to get rid of. You are tagging them now so you won't have to bother documenting them on the map you will draw of your site. Farther along in the design process, it will become obvious if more plants need to be removed.

The plants that you tagged as "remove" can go now. In fact, if you are eager to get something done in your yard, there's your first project. Just remember to keep this precious organic material on your land if possible. Now might be a good time to invest in a chipper/shredder (or cooperatively buy one with neighbors) and convert those unwanted plants into weed-suppressing mulch. One word of caution: fresh mulch, as it breaks down, will deplete nitrogen from the soil; aging the mulch for one year solves that problem. Or, even simpler, pile the plants you remove in a corner of your yard; a brush pile makes great habitat for small mammals and birds.

PLANTS: REMOVE, MOVE, OR KEEP?

REMOVE IT IF...

- It needs pesticides, synthetic fertilizer, or lots of water to survive.
- It's dead or dying.
- It's aggressive, invasive, or noxious.
- It looks bad or creates a hazard.

REMOVE OR MOVE IT IF...

- It's too large for its spot.
- It blocks a desirable view.
- It chronically has pests or disease.
- You have too many of it (in that case, remove just some).

KEEP IT IF...

- It's healthy.
- It provides food or shelter for wildlife.
- It controls erosion.
- It provides summer shade.
- It adds structure, visual balance, or beauty to the garden.
- It blocks a poor view or frames a good view.
- It provides seasonal blossoms, fruit, or foliage color exactly when and where it is needed.
- It's a good wind buffer.
- It has sentimental value or you just like it.

If you are thinking of moving a plant, you will want to find out if it's still small enough to be moved, and how well it will take to being moved. You'll also want to find out how big it will eventually get to be and what conditions it requires so that you can put it in the right place. To be environmentally responsible, you should also find out if any plants on your property are considered invasive or noxious in your state, and if any plants are conversely either endangered species themselves or host plants to an endangered animal species.

To help you access this information, you will want to find out the botanical name of the plant: the genus, species, and cultivar. Knowing that it is a viburnum is not enough—there are many viburnums, from the 2-foot-tall *Viburnum opulus* 'Nanum', the dwarf European cranberry bush, to the 12-foot-tall, 10-foot-wide *Viburnum lantana*, the wayfaring tree. Common names such as cranberry bush are not enough, either. In fact, cranberry bush is the name of two unrelated plants. A common name is better than nothing, though, because you can do an Internet search, refer to a plant encyclopedia, or go to your local cooperative extension office with that one name and your observations (such as fall leaf color, square stems or rounded, leaf veining patterns, and fruit timing), and you will most likely figure it out.

SOURCES OF
PLANT INFORMATION

TO DETERMINE THE NAME OF A PLANT:

- Take a sample or photo to your local cooperative extension office.

- If the plant is in someone's yard, knock on the front door and ask.

TO FIND OUT THE PLANT'S REQUIREMENTS AND EVENTUAL SIZE:

- Google the botanical name.

- Consult cooperative extension publications.

- Ask your garden club friends.

- Look up the plant in a plant encyclopedia.

TO FIND OUT IF THE PLANT IS DISEASED AND/OR CAN BE MOVED:

Contact a certified arborist (most will come out for free if there is a chance they will be removing tree limbs, a tree, or a large shrub).

TO FIND OUT IF A PLANT IS INVASIVE OR NOXIOUS:

- Google [your state] + "noxious weeds."

- Go to the USDA's National Invasive Species Information Center at http://www.invasivespeciesinfo.gov.

- Contact your city or county arborist, landscape architect, environmental department, or city planning department.

- Contact your county's soil and water conservation district.

TO FIND OUT IF A PLANT IS ENDANGERED OR HOSTS AN ENDANGERED ANIMAL SPECIES:

- Google [your state] + "endangered plants."

- Contact the U.S. Fish and Wildlife Service.

- Contact your city or county arborist, landscape architect, environmental department, or city planning department.

- Contact your county's soil and water conservation district.

CONSULT YOUR LOCAL COOPERATIVE EXTENSION

The Cooperative Extension System is a division of the U.S. Department of Agriculture in partnership with each state in the United States. Formed in the nineteenth century, the program allows land-grant universities to disseminate well-researched agricultural information and advice to the public. In most states, extension offices are scattered throughout the state; some even have an office in every county. This is where you can acquire extension publications, get your gardening questions answered, or sign up for a master gardener program if your state offers it.

Extension publications are a treasure trove of localized naturescaping information. A growing number of extension publications are about using water wisely, avoiding pesticides, and gardening organically. Most extensions offer detailed lists of native plants as well as drought-tolerant plants and those that can tolerate local conditions, such as sea spray.

Some state extensions host a master gardener program offering classes about the best gardening techniques and providing solid information on gardening in that area. Students pay a bargain price to be in the program and agree to volunteer a certain numbers of hours after they have completed the program, sharing their knowledge with the general public.

Names of cooperative extensions vary, but they all have "extension" in the name. An easy way to find your state's extension offices and website is to enter your state and "extension" in a search engine. You can also go to the USDA site at http://www.csrees.usda.gov/Extension/ and click on your state on the map. If you don't have web access, phone your state's land-grant university and ask for the extension service.

Scope Out Your Soil

An essential piece of information that will help you determine what you can plant is what sort of soil you have. If you are lucky, you or a former owner added organic compost and mulch (a soil-protecting layer of organic matter such as leaves or bark shavings) over many years, and you have a rich loam to work with. Most of us are not that lucky, however, and our soil is weak and virtually lifeless. There are many ways of diagnosing soil, but for naturescaping purposes you need only concern yourself with soil pH, salts, and texture.

The pH, or alkalinity/acidity of the soil, determines whether all of the nutrients present in the soil can be taken up by a plant's roots. Extremely alkaline (high pH) or acid (low pH) soil will prevent plants from taking up all available nutrients, no matter how nutrient-rich the soil is. That is, some plants will not be able to take up the nutrients; most plants that are native to that particular soil type have the ability to get what they need. Nonnative plants that have evolved under similar pH conditions usually do just fine as well. You can easily test pH with a reusable probe that you can get at a garden center or hardware store for about $20. This is a bargain compared to sending soil samples to a lab because you can get immediate results for any part of your yard anytime you want. Plant books and your cooperative extension service can help you find the plants that thrive in your soil's pH.

It is also a good idea to consider whether salts might be concentrated in your soil since high salt content can inhibit plant growth. You can usually tell that salt is a problem if by late summer your exposed soil has developed a white crust. Other signs may be that the younger leaves of your plants are yellowish, even bleached; or that your plants look like they need watering even though the soil is moist. You can also ask your cooperative extension agent if salts are a problem where you live. If you suspect that salts are a problem in your soil, you can send a sample to a soil testing lab to find out for sure. There is no cure for soil salinity, but you can plant accordingly. Also, if your land drains relatively quickly, you can leach some of the salts down into the soil and away from the root zone by watering deeply and infrequently. Salts are not as damaging to plants when the soil is dry.

Testing for nutrients is usually recommended in traditional gardening books, but you are going to be building your soil organically (simply by adding lots of organic matter), which will help your soil achieve a balance of nutrients better than adding synthetic fertilizers would. So rather than testing your soil for specific nutrients, focus your energies on adding organic material whenever possible.

You'll also want to discover your soil's texture—whether it's sandy, silty, or clayey. Most soils are a mixture of all three; your job is to find out the relative proportions. Knowing your soil's texture will help you find plants that will grow well with just what nature already provides in your yard. A good plant description will indicate if the plant tolerates drainage problems (clay soil), if it needs fast-draining soil (sandy soil), or rich soil (any type with lots of organic material). You can never change your soil's texture, but adding organic material improves its structure, which will give you healthier, faster-growing plants.

Organic matter contributed naturally to this woodland garden in the form of fallen leaves has made the soil rich enough to support a profusion of healthy plants, from eastern redbud to fothergilla. Design by Ana Hajduk.

DISCOVER YOUR SOIL'S TEXTURE

Dig a hole down to the root zone and take about a cup of soil from the bottom of the hole. If you suspect that the soil is different in the various parts of your yard due to previous practices or changes in elevation, take a sample from each area.

Dry the samples on a newspaper in the house for a few days, then run them through an old colander or wire-mesh sieve, removing roots and stones. Put each sample into a clear, straight-sided jar and add water to fill the jar, along with a few drops of dishwashing liquid. Within a few minutes the sand layer will have fallen. In the next hour, the silt layer will do the same. It takes two to three days for the clay layer to descend. Put a bookmark-size piece of paper next to the jar and mark the thickness of the layers, then measure and figure out the percentages, or just eyeball the layers and make a rough estimate.

Then mark each side of the soil textural triangle provided here with your soil's percentages of sand, silt, and clay. Draw a line from each mark to the opposite point of the triangle. The place where the three lines intersect is your soil's texture. Textures that are near the center of the triangle are relatively easy to work with; the ones nearer the points are more problematic. If you have one of these soil textures, you may need to pay particular attention to finding plants that will thrive. You can find lists online and in gardening books such as Nicola Ferguson's *Right Plant, Right Place*.

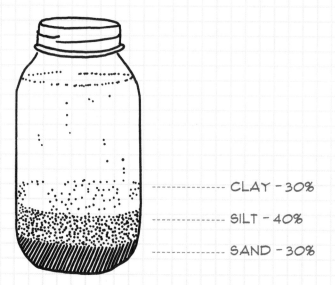

CLAY - 30%

SILT - 40%

SAND - 30%

Measure the layers of sand, silt, and clay that settle out when you combine your soil sample with water and a bit of dish soap in a clear jar. Then figure out the percentages.

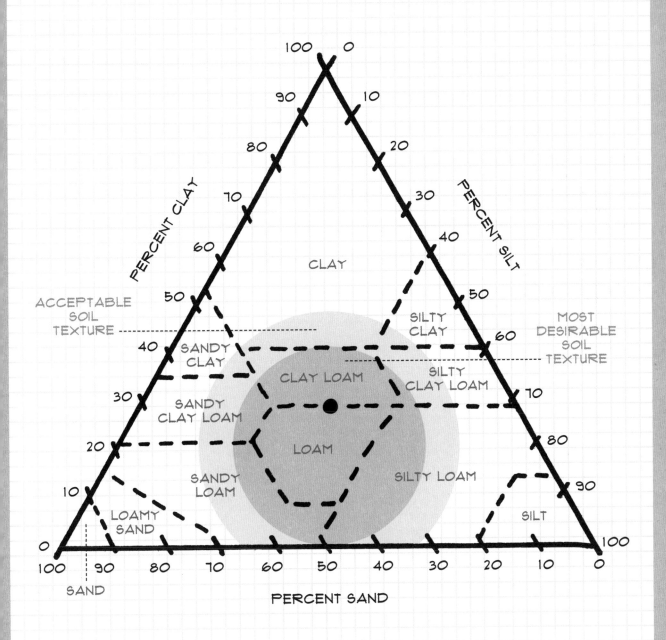

*The soil textural triangle shows the twelve major textural classes.
Mark your percentages of sand, silt, and clay on each side and draw
a line from each mark to the opposite point of the triangle. Where the
three lines intersect is your soil texture.*

GOOD NATURESCAPING CHOICES FOR EXTREME SOIL CONDITIONS

ALKALINE (HIGH PH) SOIL

Abelia grandiflora (glossy abelia)

Acer saccharum (sugar maple)

Cercis species (redbud)

Dianthus species (pinks)

Fraxinus americana (white ash)

Juniperus species (juniper)

Lavendula angustifolia (English lavender)

Platanus occidentalis (sycamore)

Salvia species (sage)

Viburnum species

ACID (LOW PH) SOIL

most conifers, including *Abies* (fir), *Larix* (larch),
Picea (spruce), and *Taxus* (yew)

Aesculus species (buckeye, horse chestnut)

Alnus species (alder)

Betula species (birch)

Camellia species

Erica species (heather)

Hydrangea species

Kalmia species (mountain laurel)

Pieris species (andromeda)

Quercus palustris (pin oak)

Rhododendron species (azalea, rhododendron)

Rubus species (raspberry, blackberry)

Skimmia species

Vaccinium species (blueberry, cranberry)

SALINE SOIL

Acer buergeranum (trident maple)

Eriobotrya japonica (loquat)

Hemerocallis species (daylily)

Lagerstroemia indica (crape myrtle)

Opuntia compressa (prickly pear cactus)

Nerium oleander (oleander)

Rosa rugosa (rugosa rose)

Trachycarpus fortunii (Chinese windmill palm)

1505

A biohabitat that offers dry shade in this Austin, Texas, front yard makes a welcoming home for native plants such as Turk's cap and Virginia creeper. Design by Scott Thurmon.

Map Your Backyard Biohabitats

In chapter 1 you started thinking about how your regional ecosystems relate to the conditions in your own yard. I suggested that nearby native plant communities might offer answers to the question of what to plant where in your garden. The idea is to recognize similar situations in your own backyard—what I call backyard biohabitats, also known as microclimates—and then select natives, or plants from another part of the country or world where ecological conditions are similar, that will thrive in those conditions.

A backyard biohabitat is an area of your yard that offers a distinct set of growing conditions. Most likely, your yard has more than one. Maybe one spot bakes in the summer sun while another is dark and moist most of the year, or perhaps one area has deep, loamy soil and another has hard-packed clay. Where the traditional gardening approach to such diversity is to homogenize and conquer, the naturescaping approach is to honor natural tendencies and plant accordingly. A biohabitat then becomes a place where plants, animals, insects, and microbes interact to create a self-sustaining system—in other words, a circle of life.

The backyard biohabitats approach is simple and straightforward. First you figure out the distinctive microclimates on your land. For each area, you decide which nearby natural ecosystem it most closely resembles. Then you populate that biohabitat with the plants that thrive in that type of natural area. It's "right plant, right place" with a twist: know your ecosystem and your biohabitats, then find the plant that nature would choose to fit the conditions your yard offers.

Recognize microclimates and corresponding plant communities

Let's say that an area of your yard is sunny most of the day, shielded from the summer sun only in early morning and late afternoon. It is currently irrigated lawn but you want it to be unirrigated shrubs, perennials, and ornamental grasses. In the Midwest, the ecological community corresponding to this

scenario would be a prairie. You would therefore populate this area of your yard with plants that thrive in prairies: grasses and wildflowers. If you live in California, the ecological community corresponding to this scenario would be an oak savannah, and some of the plants found thriving there would be monkeyflowers, manzanitas, and live oaks.

Or say you have standing water in part of your yard at certain times of the year. Your corresponding ecosystem for that area might be freshwater marsh. Once you know this, you'll be able to populate that area with plants that will revel in this situation—iris, sedge, and cattails—rather than looking at it as a drainage problem requiring expensive grading, piping, and grates.

An organized way to match plants to your backyard biohabitats is to first create a biohabitats map of your property and then chart each biohabitat, noting its characteristics, the name of the nearby ecosystem that most closely resembles this biohabitat, and the plants that naturally grow there. This will give you a great starter list of natives that will thrive in your garden. Later in this chapter you'll add on to that.

Create a biohabitats map

Now is the time to create a map that shows how your yard looks right now minus the things you plan to remove. With this map, you will have an accurate basis for making design decisions. For now, you will use a copy of this base map to note the biohabitats in your yard. There are a few ways to create this map, a couple of which require no drawing skills.

An easy way to create your base map is to use Google Maps to get and print out an aerial photo of your property. This approach works if you have very little tree cover on your property; one big tree can obscure your entire backyard. Blow up the satellite photo to 8-1/2 by 11 inches and find something you can measure on the photo such as the edge of a roof or driveway. From that measurement you can figure out the scale of your photo. For instance, if your front fence is 1 inch long on the map and

PLANTS THAT THRIVE IN DRY SUN

Acacia species

Achillea species (yarrow)

Agave species

Arbutus unedo (strawberry tree)

Arctostaphyllos species (manzanita)

Berberis species (barberry)

Cistus species (rockrose)

Cotinus coggygria (smokebush)

Lantana species

Lavandula species (lavender)

Oenothera species (evening primrose)

Penstemon species (beard tongue)

Salvia species (sage)

Sedum species (stonecrop)

Yucca species

PLANTS THAT THRIVE IN MOIST SHADE

Acer rubrum (red maple)

Adiantum species (maidenhair ferns)

Aquilegia species (columbine)

Betula nigra (river birch)

Cercis species (redbud)

Cornus canadensis (bunchberry)

Cornus sericea (red osier dogwood)

Hosta species

Mertensia virginica (Virginia bluebells)

Primula species (primrose)

Rhododendron species
(rhododendrons and azaleas)

you go out and measure it and find that it's 8 feet long in reality, your scale is 1 inch = 8 feet (or 1/8 inch = 1 foot). This is a good working scale. You may need to magnify the photo even more to get to this scale; any blueprint shop should have a printer big enough to make the blowup for you.

You can also start with the plat map of your property (which you received when you purchased your house and which is probably available at your assessor's office or website as well). You'll need to magnify the plat map to get to a good working scale and add structures to it, but it will show you the shape of your land. If you like to draw, another alternative is to follow the instructions here to draw your own base map to scale.

Pink lady's slipper, moss, and skunk cabbage flourish in a moist woodland biohabitat.
Coastal Maine Botanical Garden.

DRAW YOUR PROPERTY TO SCALE

YOU WILL NEED:

large clipboard—or any sturdy board—about 2 feet square

grid paper (one 17 x 34-inch sheet, or more if your property is larger)

masking tape

sharp #2 pencils with pencil-top erasers (white erasers are best)

sharp colored pencils (eight or so)

directional compass

vinyl 100- or 200-foot measuring tape

metal or plastic 10-foot measuring tape

1/8-inch gridded vellum (one 22 x 34-inch sheet, or a larger sheet if your property is larger)

drawing compass with pencil attached
tracing paper (sheets or roll)

FOLLOW THESE STEPS TO DRAW YOUR PROPERTY TO SCALE:

1. Make a rough sketch in pencil on grid paper.

2. Measure your property and add the measurements to the sketch.

3. Working from the sketch, draw the base map in pencil on gridded vellum.

SKETCH

First create a rough sketch of your yard, large enough so you can add measurements later. This sketch does not need to be perfect; just try to make things proportional to each other. You can also start with the plat map of your property and magnify it in order to note measurements on it.

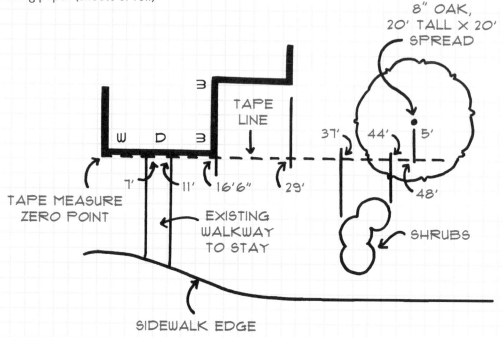

By aligning your tape measure with a side of the house, you are working off a grid so your measurements are accurate. Mark the measurements at various key points, such as where the tapeline crosses a path.

Go outside with a large sheet of gridded paper (or your magnified plat map) taped to a board and sketch the plan view of the house and your land. Draw in property lines, fences, paths, patios, decks, tree trunks, shrub masses, and any other landscape feature that will be staying. You can do it freehand (the gridded lines help) or you can use a ruler to help you. It does not need to be pretty.

MEASURE

Then add the measurements to your sketch, starting with the house. Put the end of your measuring tape at one corner (if you don't have a helper to hold this end, you can put a screwdriver through the end loop and jam it into the ground) and draw the tape along the wall and beyond, keeping in line with the house wall. Take the tape measure all the way to the edge of the project (fence, sidewalk, or property line).

Walk along the tape measure and note on your sketch the distance from the corner at various key points, such as the end of the house and where the tapeline crosses a path. I mark where windows and doors begin and end, but as a shortcut you can simply take the house's corner-to-corner measurements, then draw a W at the approximate center of each window and a D where a door is. Don't worry about being perfectly accurate; landscape drawings are at such a large scale that you needn't be more accurate than the nearest 6-inch mark. For each new tapeline that you lay, document it with a new color of pencil; otherwise, your drawing will become difficult to read.

For trees, note where an imaginary line from the tree trunk perpendicular to the tapeline would meet the tapeline. Then, with a shorter tape measure, measure the length of that imaginary line and make a note of it on your sketch. For each tree, note (1) the trunk diameter, (2) its name, if you know it, (3) its approximate height, and (4) its spread (also known as the "dripline"). If you have trees

that are far from any tapelines, simply take measurements from two known points, maybe a house corner (point A) and the edge of a doorway (point B). Later on, when you are drawing up your base map, use a compass to draw two arcs from these points and place the tree where they intersect.

For a mass of shrubbery that will stay, show it as a cloud shape on your sketch and indicate the start and finish of the shrub mass on the tapeline. For a patio that will remain, show where the tape measure crosses the edge of the patio (if it does). When you've finished taking measurements from the first side of the house, repeat this process for each of the other sides. Get out your directional compass, find north, and mark it on your plan.

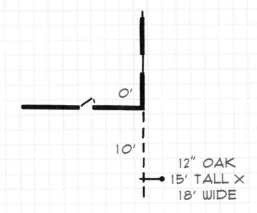

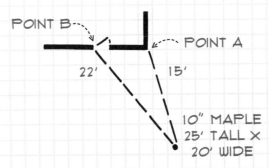

There are two ways to locate a tree on your plan: measure from a tapeline extended from a wall of the house, or measure from two known points. Also note the trunk diameter, name, height, and spread.

DRAW

Now draw your base map—the map that will be the basis of other drawings. This does not have to be fancy, but it does need to be all in proportion; that's why you've done the measuring. Work at a clean, perfectly flat rectangular kitchen table or desk. Use 1/8-inch gridded vellum, a tough archival quality paper available at art supply stores or copy shops that is see-through and pencil-erasable. The grids are visible to you as you draw but they don't copy. They are great guidelines for writing notes and making sure that the right angles of your house and other rectilinear shapes on your drawings are in line. Plus they enable you to scale your drawing so that 1/8 inch on your drawing represents 1 foot in the real world, an easy scale to work with.

Tape your vellum to the table. Start by drawing the house footprint—that is, where the exterior wall meets the ground plane—with your #2 pencil. Translate the measurements in feet on your rough sketch into measurements in inches on your map by dividing the number of feet by 8. In other words, each inch on the map will represent 8 feet in the real world. Make sure that you place the house on the paper so that you will be able to show the entire property.

Show anything overhead, such as a roof eave or an arbor, as a dashed line. Show a tree trunk as a dot the size of the trunk (that is, if the trunk is 12 inches in diameter, the dot would be 1/8 inch in diameter on your drawing). Show shrub masses with a solid line in a cloud shape. Label all the plants. If you don't know the name, write what you do know, such as "evergreen" or "maybe a magnolia."

As a final touch, transfer the north arrow to your new drawing. Write down the scale (1/8 inch = 1 foot), the name or address of the property, your name, and the date. Make a few copies of this map on regular white bond paper; you'll be using a copy to make your biohabitats map and you'll use copies later to help you make informed decisions in your final design.

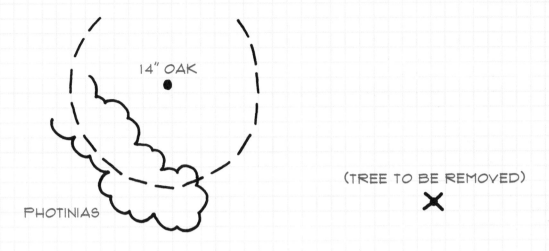

14" OAK

(TREE TO BE REMOVED)
X

PHOTINIAS

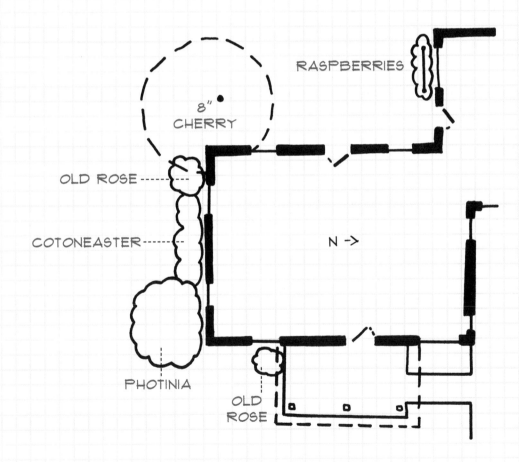

RASPBERRIES

8"
CHERRY

OLD ROSE - - - - -

COTONEASTER - - - - -

N →

PHOTINIA

OLD
ROSE

*The base map shows everything that won't change, drawn to
scale so all the proportions are correct.*

Take a copy of your base map and tape a piece of tracing paper over this sheet. On the tracing paper, use colored pencils to outline the various biohabitats in your yard—zones that differ from the adjacent zones in terms of sun exposure, soil type, or natural moisture content of the soil. For example, you might have an area that never gets direct sun, where the soil is dry between rainfalls. That zone would be different from an area that also gets no sun but is situated at the bottom of a hill and is always moist. Give each biohabitat a number or name (such as RF for riparian forest).

This naturescape features two backyard biohabitats in close proximity—a stony ledge planted with drought-tolerant thyme, sedum, and creeping oregano and a wet area planted with native goldenrod and daylilies.

Outline areas of the following types (some of these areas may overlap):

- Sunny: six hours or more of direct sunlight per day in the summer (yellow)
- Hot spots: where the sun is a problem in the summer (orange)
- Shady: less than one hour of direct sun per day in the summer (green)
- Windy: exposed parts of the yard where it is unpleasant to be on windy days (light blue)
- Wet soil: where the ground has seasonal standing water or is seasonally mucky (blue)
- Dry soil: where the soil is dry, perhaps even cracked, in the summer (brown)
- Sloping: where the slope is mild and walkable (arrow pointing downward, blue)
- Very sloping: where steps might be needed, if a path ran through there (double arrows pointing downward, purple)
- Steep: unwalkable as is (triple arrows pointing downward, black)

Make a chart

Now you're going to make a chart listing each plant zone you've identified on your map. List the plant zone name or number, its characteristics (such as sun exposure, soil moisture, and soil type), the name of the nearby ecosystem that most closely resembles this plant zone (draw on what you learned on your local hikes and through Internet research here), and the plants that naturally grow there. One way to get this latter information is to Google the ecosystem name + [your state] + "plants." I rely on government or university websites for credible ecosystem information rather than nurseries, nonprofits, or chat sites. Most publications about an ecosystem include a listing or discussion of the plants that grow there.

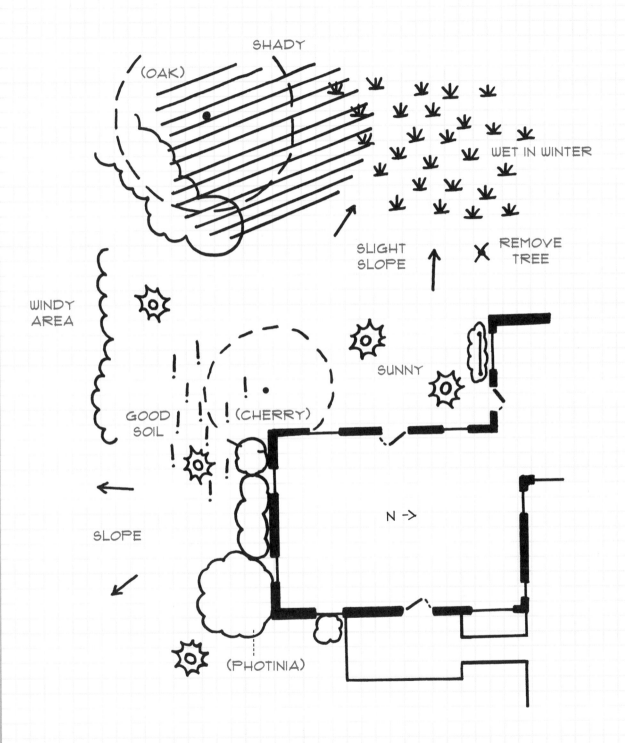

The biohabits map documents natural features of your yard such as sun and wind patterns, soils, and slopes.

WORKSHEET 3: BACKYARD BIOHABITATS CHART

FILL OUT THIS CHART FOR EACH ZONE IN YOUR YARD,
FOLLOWING THE EXAMPLE SHOWN HERE.

ZONE	RF
Characteristics	Shady all year, low, water drains to here, a little moist in the summer
Corresponding ecosystem	Riparian Forest
Plants in that ecosystem	Lady fern (Athyrium filix-femina) Skunk cabbage (Symplocarpus foetidus) Thimbleberry (Rubus parviflorus) Salmonberry (Rubus spectabilis)

ZONE	
Characteristics	
Corresponding ecosystem	
Plants in that ecosystem	

ZONE	
Characteristics	
Corresponding ecosystem	
Plants in that ecosystem	

ZONE	
Characteristics	
Corresponding ecosystem	
Plants in that ecosystem	

ZONE

Characteristics

Corresponding ecosystem

Plants in that ecosystem

ZONE

Characteristics

Corresponding ecosystem

Plants in that ecosystem

ZONE

Characteristics

Corresponding ecosystem

Plants in that ecosystem

ZONE

Characteristics

Corresponding ecosystem

Plants in that ecosystem

What would nature do with this piece of land baking in the sun?

Perhaps populate it with sun lovers like purple coneflower and black-eyed Susan, along with native grasses.
Design by Richter & Cegan Landscape Architects.

Start Your Plant List

Now you are ready to start your plant list. Your plant list is the palette that you, the artist, will work from when creating your naturescape. Make a separate section for each plant zone in your yard. You can do this on a computer spreadsheet or on the worksheet provided here. Enter the name of each plant from your biohabitats chart, its eventual height and spread, seasonal features, and any notes. At this point, the idea is to generate a good selection of plant matches to choose from. Later, when you finalize your naturescape design, you will research purchasing information and the exact number of each kind of plant that you need.

Categories of plants to include

Start your list with the plants listed on your backyard biohabitats chart. You can also add some appropriate nonnatives to the list as well. Naturescaping is not just about native plants. These kinds of plants can also be part of your naturescape:

❧ *Appropriates*—This is what I call nonnative plants that have grown up under similar conditions to those on your land. These plants may be from far-flung areas of the world, but they possess the characteristics to survive in your yard with little help from you. For example, if you live in a Mediterranean climate (characterized by mild winters and hot, dry summers), appropriate plants for your yard might come from Australia, South Africa, Turkey, Chile, or Spain. If you live with cold winters and warm, moist summers, your appropriates might come from England and Japan. Appropriates are a wonderful way to expand your seasons and introduce interesting flowers, foliage, or form into your garden.

❧ *Multifunctional plants*—The idea that plants should serve a number of uses rather than being purely ornamental is central to permaculture, an approach to gardening in which the land is regarded as a unified whole. Bamboo is the classic example. It can be used to create a quick-growing screen to block a bad view or give privacy. The restful sound of its leaves quivering in the wind makes it a natural material to use for a meditation grove. It provides leaves and twigs for birds to make nests from, as well as a safe hiding place for many species of birds. The canes can be used to build trellises to support twining vines and even cherry tomato bushes. It can also be planted on a steep slope to provide erosion control. Other plants can be chosen for their medicinal properties, their ability to fix nitrogen in the soil, or their provision of seeds or berries for birds, to give just a few examples.

❧ *Edibles*—Arguably, the most useful plants are the ones that give us food. When you eat from your own backyard, you avoid the use of fossil fuels that go into transporting, fertilizing, and eradicating pests on conventionally grown crops, and you are not part of the agribusiness monster that is responsible for depleted soils, contaminated groundwater, and species extinctions. My favorite edibles are low-care but also ornamental. In the right place (and that includes the right part of the country), many edibles are low-maintenance. Check your local extension publications or ask knowledgeable nursery personnel for the right cultivars for your region, preferences, and needs. They will also have information on the most disease-resistant cultivars available.

❧ *Favorites*—Then there are the plants that are not native, appropriate, or even useful. You may have listed them under "plant preferences" in your wants and needs worksheet, or perhaps they keep showing up in the garden photos you clip—plants that you love even though you shouldn't. A sensible alternative to these heartbreakers is to note their characteristics and find an appropriate plant that shares these characteristics. If you see a lot of large-leaf perennials such as hosta or bergenia in your photos, yet they don't grow well (without constant care) where you live, you could satisfy your desire with another big-leaf perennial, one that thrives in your climate without all that drama. Your local nursery is a great place to find such a fine specimen; just walking around will probably lead you to one in no time. Staff members of any good nursery will be happy to help you find alternatives as well; they know their plants well and love challenges like that.

A dry, sunny rock outcrop will naturally support
creeping rosemary, thyme, stonecrop, pinks,
and daisies. Design by Big Red Sun.

Colorful plants for full sun and well-drained soil
include bright yellow buckwheat (lower left),
pink and purple penstemon, deep purple lavender,
and yellow mullein (upper right).
Denver Botanic Garden.

WORKSHEET 4: **PRELIMINARY PLANT LIST**

LIST PLANTS FOR EACH ZONE IN YOUR YARD, FOLLOWING THE EXAMPLE SHOWN HERE.

PLANT ZONE	RF
Plant name(s)	Lady fern (Athyrium filix-femina)
Height (spread)	4 ft. tall, 2-3 ft. wide
Seasonal features	Lacy fern foliage (spring, summer, fall)
Notes	Dies down in winter

PLANT ZONE	
Plant name(s)	
Height (spread)	
Seasonal features	
Notes	

PLANT ZONE	
Plant name(s)	
Height (spread)	
Seasonal features	
Notes	

PLANT ZONE	
Plant name(s)	
Height (spread)	
Seasonal features	
Notes	

PLANT ZONE	
Plant name(s)	
Height (spread)	
Seasonal features	
Notes	

PLANT ZONE

Plant name(s)

Height (spread)

Seasonal features

Notes

PLANT ZONE

Plant name(s)

Height (spread)

Seasonal features

Notes

PLANT ZONE

Plant name(s)

Height (spread)

Seasonal features

Notes

PLANT ZONE

Plant name(s)

Height (spread)

Seasonal features

Notes

PLANT ZONE

Plant name(s)

Height (spread)

Seasonal features

Notes

EDIBLES THAT ARE
ALSO ORNAMENTAL

TREES

apple, pear, Asian pear

bay

cherry, almond

English walnut

fig (best as a multi-trunk tree)

hazelnut

olive

orange, lemon, grapefruit, lime, kumquat

pawpaw

peach, nectarine

persimmon

plum, pluot, apricot

pomegranate

quince (fruiting)

VINES

grapes

peas

SHRUBS AND SUBSHRUBS

aronia

blueberries

highbush cranberry

honeyberry

lingonberry

pistachio

rosemary

GROUND COVERS

strawberry

thyme

HERBS THAT LOOK GOOD
TUCKED IN ANYWHERE

basil

marjoram

oregano

parsley

sage

FLOWERS YOU CAN EAT
(KIDS LOVE THESE)

bee balm

chives

garlic

impatiens

nasturtiums

onions

peas

pineapple guava

pot marigolds (*Calendula*)

squash blossoms, including zucchini and pumpkin

sunflowers

violets

LUSH LEAVES AND
COLORFUL FRUIT

chard

cherry tomatoes

hot peppers

kale

rhubarb

Fruits and vegetables can be a beautiful part of your naturescape. Here broccoli and runner beans mingle with clematis and boxwoods.

Grasses lend movement and also produce striking seed heads that can decorate the yard in winter when not much else is of interest.

Runner beans trained on a wire arch provide food as well as an attractive frame for a view out the French doors.

A naturescape celebrates the season.

Diversity and your plant list

Your naturescape will not be a monoculture (a mass of one plant species, like a cornfield, an endless expanse of lawn, or a big tomato patch). Because you have been observant of nature, your new yard will most likely reflect the inherent diversity of the places you have visited. And because of it, you will have a year-round landscape: a garden that celebrates the seasons and has something interesting to reveal each day. Colorful fall foliage, winter berries and evergreen boughs, spring leaves and blossoms, and summer fruits and flowers will decorate your year.

Even if you live in an area with indistinct seasons, you can choose plants that bring out their best at different times of the year—native and appropriate plants that reflect the changes. In the fall, it will be the leaves showing their reds, oranges, and yellows as they drift to the ground. In the winter, plants with striking branches, deep-green foliage, or contrasting berries come to the fore. In the spring, deciduous trees and shrubs begin to show their pale green leaves, and pastel bulbs may appear below. Summer brings the riot of color with flowers, fruits, berries, and even the foliage of some perennials.

One way of achieving year-round beauty is to create a month-by-month graph of the plants you plan to use and what seasonal feature each plant will bring. Then choose the plants that have more than one season of interest. Taking walks to a nearby natural area in each season to see what is looking good can give you ideas.

But diversity is not just about aesthetic pleasure; incorporating diversity into your naturescape will help your garden stave off an infestation, weather an ice storm, or endure a drought. Some of the members may perish, but the remaining ones will flourish—and will fill in the voids. That is the real beauty of a naturescape.

ELEMENTS OF A DIVERSE NATURESCAPE

evergreen trees · deciduous trees

evergreen shrubs · deciduous shrubs

perennials that die down in the winter

year-round perennials
(only in temperate regions)

vines · grasses · ferns · bulbs · herbs

fruits and nuts

CHAPTER 3 HOMEWORK:
PUT THE RIGHT PLANT IN THE RIGHT PLACE

- ☐ Inventory the plants you already have and decide which should stay and which need to be moved or removed.

- ☐ Determine your soil's pH and texture.

- ☐ Create a base map of your property and on a tracing paper overlay, map your backyard biohabitats.

- ☐ Complete worksheet 3, "Backyard Biohabits Chart."

- ☐ Complete worksheet 4, "Preliminary Plant List."

- ☐ Ensure that your list includes a good variety of plants for diversity and year-round interest.

chapter four

WELCOME WILDLIFE

Attract birds, small animals, and beneficial insects by providing a welcoming habitat and rely on them to do the pest patrol.

By choosing to plant natives in your garden, you will already have gone a long way toward providing food and habitat for wild creatures that are being pushed toward extinction by a growing human population. As entomology professor Douglas Tallamy points out in Bringing Nature Home, *our wildlife is increasingly dependent on the landscapes and gardens that we create, since uncontrolled expansion of human settlements is crowding wildlife off of wildlands. "Unless we modify the places we live, work, and play to meet not only our own needs but the needs of other species as well, nearly all species of wildlife native to the United States will disappear forever," warns Tallamy.*

As just one example, because of habitat loss many bird populations—a long list that includes hawks, swallows, wood thrushes, and wrens—have been decreasing at an average rate of 1 percent per year since 1966. In other words, these species will have experienced a 50 percent population reduction from 1966 levels by 2016. Tallamy goes on to assert that "most species could live quite nicely with humans if their most basic ecological needs were met." Sara Stein makes a similar point in *Noah's Garden*, urging us to welcome all wildlife into our yards to save creatures from the rising tides of habitat loss and pesticide persistence.

In this chapter you will take the next step in thinking about elements to include in your naturescape design by considering what the ecological needs of wild creatures are. A naturescape seeks to preserve habitat for the creatures we share our region with. By welcoming everybody—microbes, mycelium, mushrooms, moss, mammals, algae, insects, spiders, amphibians, birds—we can ensure that no one species gets out of control or faces extinction in the long run. But what about those unchecked populations, the ones whose predators are not around for one reason or another, such as deer, raccoons, rabbits, geese, slugs, and snails? What to do when you find these "pests" wreaking havoc in your garden is also discussed in this chapter.

Plan to Meet the Four Basic Needs

The four basic needs of wildlife are water, food, shelter, and space. As a living ecosystem, a naturescape is a place where a clean water source is safely accessible, where the perfect source of protein is available exactly when needed in the creature's life cycle, where safe shelters are easily found or created with minimal energy expenditure, and where a creature can roam—or its population can grow—without being crowded into smaller and smaller spaces.

We will consider each of these needs, and how your naturescape can provide for them, in turn. First, though, it's essential to acknowledge that good soil is the alpha and omega of a healthy ecosystem. Good soil leads to lush plant growth, the origin of all forms of wildlife habitat, from treetops for eagles to decaying bark for beetles. Good soil leads to copious production of flowers and fruits, the raw materials for healthy insect, bird, amphibian, and mammal populations. And the soil itself is host to grubs and such—needed protein for these higher fauna. We will return to the importance of good soil—and how to build good soil in your naturescape—later in the book.

A NATURESCAPE THAT WELCOMES WILDLIFE OFFERS

clean, accessible water

an abundant and diverse food supply, enough for every creature at every life stage

structurally intricate physical niches (habitat)

access to other similar ecosystems nearby (space)

Brush piles, fallen leaves, dead wood, and upright snags provide habitat for birds and bugs. Here a bald eagle perches on a snag in the Deschutes National Forest in Oregon.

This recirculating fountain makes a pleasant sound as it drips down the sides of the vase, moistening the rocks below. Butterflies enjoy perching on the rocks and slurping the water, and small amphibians like to hide among the rocks and eat any aquatic insects that emerge. Design by Westover Landscape Design.

Clean, accessible water

Water is an amazing attractor of wildlife—not only raccoons and deer but also dragonflies, songbirds, turtles, and frogs. How you bring water into your garden is limited only by your imagination and wallet. The important thing is that the water stays fresh: making the water drip, move, or splash is the best way to do this without resorting to life-killing chlorine. And if you are lucky enough to have a natural source of water on your land such as a stream or wetland, preserve it and allow native plants to grow tall along its edges.

A birdbath is a simple way to attract birds, squirrels, and chipmunks. There are two basic kinds: pedestal and ground-level baths. Birds such as chickadees and finches are attracted to pedestal baths, while other birds and small mammals visit the ground-level baths because they more closely resemble a natural spring or pond. With one of each, you can get all kinds of species visiting your yard. Above all, if you do decide to have a birdbath, make a pledge to keep it sanitary by changing the water daily and cleaning it once a week; otherwise don't have a birdbath at all.

Birdbath basics

- Locate pedestal baths near shrubs or low tree branches so that birds can quickly evade predators from the sky.

- Locate ground-level baths where cats or other creeping predators can't sneak up on the bathers; 10 to 15 inches from a hiding place is a good idea.

- Birds like to wade into the water so a graduated edge is best.

- Birds will only use a bath with shallow water (no more than 2 or 3 inches deep).

- Birds dislike slippery surfaces, so add rocks or even bathtub decals to your bath to make it more hospitable.

- Locate your birdbath in the shade; this, along with frequent washings, will also keep algae growth in check.

- Keep it clean! To avoid bird diseases and death, change the water daily. Brush-clean the bath weekly with a nine-to-one water-bleach solution.

HELP THE HONEYBEES

In a phenomenon researchers first dubbed colony collapse disorder (CCD) in late 2006, honeybee colonies in North America, Europe, and Asia have been suffering the sudden and widespread death of worker bees. Because honeybees pollinate so many flowering food crops—including apples, citrus fruits, and nuts—the bees' disappearance is significant to the human food supply. The cause of the disorder appears to be viral and fungal, but scientists are still searching for definitive answers.

Meanwhile, there are a couple of things home gardeners can do to help the plight of the honeybees. First, use no pesticides. Common garden pesticides kill bees, just like agricultural chemicals do, and garden pesticides don't necessarily carry warning labels stating this fact. Second, expand bee habitat by planting flowering fruit and nut trees and well as favorites like bee balm, clover, and borage. Leave part of your garden wild so bees can gather nectar from flowering weeds like dandelions.

Birds seem to like drippers and misters. A simple dripper can be made from a large plastic soda bottle pricked at the bottom and filled with water. Hang it over a birdbath and allow it to drip in (the bottle will need to be filled daily). Many birds, but especially hummingbirds, enjoy misters. A mister attaches to your garden hose and lets a fine spray into the air. You can usually find misters (and drippers) where birdbaths are sold.

A backyard pond is a bigger commitment, of money, installation time, and maintenance, but is an incredible animal attractor. Ponds can range from a simple depression in the land to an elaborate display of waterfalls, spillways, and multiple pools. If you decide to build a wildlife pond, make it as natural as possible by not using a pond liner; instead, pack the soil below and line it with rocks and sand. Add submersible plants that are native to your area, and provide some shallow spots to give turtles, frogs, and toads places to lay eggs. If you want turtles, make them an island: a bit of log that sticks out of the water so they can sun themselves and plop back into the water.

Amphibians such as frogs, turtles, newts, and salamanders are fun to have in the yard, and they are voracious insect eaters. Fortunately, they can be found in almost any wet or moist naturalistic situation—under leaves, rocks, underbrush, rotting logs. Just add water to any part of your naturescape and you are bound to get some amphibians (which is another good reason to disconnect your house's downspouts and redirect the water into your yard).

A diverse and abundant food supply

Food for animals in your naturescape can—and, in my opinion, *should*—be entirely provided by plants rather than feeders. You can achieve this by planting a variety of plants, mostly natives. In a working ecosystem, native plants, insects, birds, amphibians, and mammals have grown to depend on and repel each other in just the right measure so that no species dominates or dies out. There are such amazing intricacies in each ecosystem that we humans will likely never understand them all, much less recreate them. But we can plant native to help save our functional ecosystems and their healthy wildlife populations.

Natives have the arcane ability to provide the right food for native insects and animals at the exact time when it is needed. All fauna have specific nutritional requirements, requirements that change throughout their life cycles and with the seasons. The plants that evolved with them—native plants—provide the right leaf mass, nectar, seeds, grains, and fruits at exactly the right point in the life cycle of the hungry critter. Most exotics cannot do this. Up to 90 percent of all leaf-eating insects, which provide essential protein to birds, bats, and others, eat only one species of native plant and don't adapt to aliens.

Sadly, we usually don't hear about symbiotic flora and fauna until one of these populations is dying to the point of potential extinction. Such was the case with the Fender's blue butterfly, which is endemic to the Willamette Valley of Oregon and was once thought extinct—it was found only in butterfly collections from the 1920s and 1930s—until a live one was discovered in 1989, launching investigation of its life cycle. It was found that the Fender's blue relies on only one species of lupine, the Kincaid's lupine, as the host plant during its larval stage. But the Kinkaid's lupine has experienced an extreme loss of habitat since pre-Columbian days and was listed as endangered in 2000. The butterfly has evolved with the lupine and depends on it for the exact nutrition it needs at precisely the time it is needed. When meadows of lupines became farms and houses, the world nearly lost this little blue beauty.

This is just one example of how native fauna rely on native flora: right time, right shelter, right food source, right type of nutrition. As naturescapers we can do our best to assist them by providing a diversity of plants and choosing natives when feasible. The lists of food-source plants in this chapter suggest various genera. Depending on the part of the country you live in, you can probably

PLANTS THAT FEED BUTTERFLIES, MOTHS, CATERPILLARS, AND BENEFICIAL INSECTS

TREES

Betula species (birch)

Cornus florida (flowering dogwood)

Fraxinus species (ash)

Malus (crabapple)

Populus species (cottonwood, poplars)

Prunus species (cherry, plum)

Quercus species (oak)

Salix species (willows)

SHRUBS AND SHRUBLIKE PLANTS

Agave species

Cephalanthus occidentalis (buttonbush)

Hebe species

Lavandula species (lavender)

Ribes species (currant)

Syringa species (lilac)

Vaccinium species (blueberry, cranberry, dilberry, deerberry)

Viburnum species

Yucca species

PERENNIALS, ANNUALS, GRASSES, AND GROUND COVERS

Asclepias species (milkweed, butterfly weed)

Aster species

Cosmos species

Echinacea species (coneflower)

Eupatorium species (Joe-Pye weed)

Festuca species (fescue)

Monarda species (bee balm)

Rudbeckia species (black-eyed Susan)

Salvia species (sage)

Sedum species (stonecrop)

Viola species (violet)

find a native species of these plants for your naturescape. For example, if you live in the south Texas plains, the live oak (*Quercus virginiana*) might be a good choice for your yard. If you live in western Florida, you might choose the dahoon holly (*Ilex cassine*) and Darrow's blueberry (*Vaccinium darrowii*) to provide berries for birds. If you live in Massachusetts, you might want to plant a northern red oak (*Quercus rubra*) or a pitch pine (*Pinus rigida*).

PLANTS WITH BERRIES FOR BIRDS

TREES

Amelanchier species (serviceberry)

Crataegus species (hawthorn)

Malus species (crabapple)

Prunus lusitanica (Portugal laurel)

Sambucus species (elderberry)

Sorbus species (mountain ash)

SHRUBS

Aronia species (chokeberry)

Berberis species (barberry)

Cotoneaster species

Euonymus species

Ilex species (holly)

Ligustrum species (privet)

Mahonia species (Oregon grape)

Pyracantha species

Vaccinium species (blueberries, huckleberries)

Viburnum tinus, V. davidii

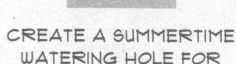

CREATE A SUMMERTIME WATERING HOLE FOR BUTTERFLIES

YOU WILL NEED:

heat-absorbing stones

sea salt

clean sand

a mister or hose with mister attachment

black plastic landscape cloth (impervious to water)

Make a shallow depression, 3 to 5 square feet in area. Place the landscape cloth in the depression, turned up at the edges so it holds water. Spread the rocks evenly on the cloth. Sprinkle with the salt and the sand. Mist the mixture and watch the butterflies come. You can make the place extra appealing by having some or all of the rocks in the sun so the butterflies can dry their wings. A nearby mud bog will attract them as well; they extract nutrients from the mud. Also, a banana (or other fruit fly attractor) will provide them an extra treat: an all-you-can-eat fruit fly bar.

A native tiger swallowtail gathers nectar from native perennials bee balm and coneflower in a Northeast garden.
Natives provide nutrients and shelter exactly when it is needed in the butterfly's life cycle.
Design by Richard Bergmann, AIA, ASLA.

This diverse garden features plants that attract beneficial insects, allowing for organic cultivation of roses in the border; plants such as coneflowers to provide seeds for the birds later in the season; and nectar sources such as bee balm for hummingbirds and bees. The butterfly house on the pole is mostly ornamental. Design by Natureworks.

THE TRUTH ABOUT BIRD FEEDERS

Many people enjoy putting up feeders for the local birds and keeping them stocked with suet or seeds. Is this a good idea? Actually, it's not, unless feeders are kept scrupulously clean. Otherwise, they can become a home for disease-causing organisms. For example, the disease-causing *Trichomonad* protozoan can live for up to five days in dropped seeds and hulls.

This same pathogen can live several hours in water. In recent years, state fish and wildlife biologists have put out warnings about backyard feeders because specific bird populations were decreasing in alarming numbers.

"The plain fact is that wild birds do not need to be fed, and they are quite capable of finding what they need to sustain them in the natural world," says Colin Gillin, president of the American Association of Wildlife Veterinarians. "Also, feeders can keep migrating birds in an inappropriate seasonal habitat too long, making the flight to warmer winter habitats more treacherous the closer inclement weather approaches." If you are concerned about this, consult your local fish and wildlife department or cooperative extension office for information on your local bird populations.

If you do decide to maintain a feeder, make sure you keep it clean. Gillin gives this advice:

Disinfect once or twice a month. Wearing rubber gloves, immerse your seed feeder in a nine-to-one water-bleach solution and then rinse it thoroughly. In the presence of outbreaks (check with your local fish and wildlife department if you suspect something is amiss), stop feeding for at least a month so the sick birds will stop contaminating your feeder, and if you start feeding again, disinfect twice as often.

Discard old seed and hulls. When you clean your feeder, get rid of the old seeds. A blow-dryer works well for this. Rake or sweep up any uneaten hulls on the ground.

Avoid overcrowding. If possible, provide more than one feeder and spread them out. (Another solution would be to avoid the feeders and scatter the seeds throughout the yard.) Crowding only expedites the spread of disease, so give the birds variety and plenty of room.

Do not use wood or platform feeders. Pathogens harbor in the wood no matter how much you clean it. Platform feeders allow the birds to concentrate where they are feeding and to defecate in close proximity to their food.

Physical niches (habitat)

Every animal has its niche, its favorite hidey-hole or perch with a view. Nature provides an abundance of physical niches, from the mucky clay soil that the butterflies love to the highest treetop favored by the bald eagle. Ecologists talk about these habitats in terms of structural diversity or intricacy. You can think about your naturescape in terms of structural diversity, too. The more different kinds of habitats you provide, the more diverse will be the insect and animal life that visits.

In the case of birds, ornithologists have categorized the vertical niches—ground, herb, shrub, tree, and upper canopy—and the birds that typically occupy these sites. If an ecosystem—or a garden—does not have that perfect niche, that bird will fly by, continuing its search for what it needs. You can make sure that you are welcoming as many birds as possible by providing plants at every vertical niche.

An array of native birds—including chickadees, turkey vultures, kestrels, wood ducks, bluebirds, and martins—love to inhabit nesting boxes, either year-round or for nesting purposes only. Natural cavities are no longer as available to them because hardwood forests are disappearing and the practice of taking down dead or decaying trees is becoming more widespread. Wildlife specialists encourage homeowners to put up nesting boxes as a way of helping out these and other native species.

STRUCTURALLY INTRICATE ELEMENTS THAT ATTRACT WILDLIFE

rock piles, brush piles, woodpiles

flat objects, such as pieces of plywood or garbage-can lids

snags (standing dead trees), fallen trees

thickets and hedgerows

freshwater ponds, creeks, or streams

muddy or seasonally mucky areas

TOP TEN TREES THAT FEED AND SHELTER WILDLIFE

Acer species (maple, box elder)

Betula species (birch)

Carya species (hickory)

Malus species (crabapple)

Pinus species (pine)

Populus species (cottonwood, poplar)

Prunus species (cherry and plum)

Quercus species (oak)

Salix species (willow)

Ulmus species (elm)

Providing cover where it is otherwise rare, such as in the desert or in a sea of green lawns, is essential for the survival of wildlife. This native planting behind homes in Tucson provides cover for jackrabbits, foxes, and cactus wrens. Design by Civano Nursery.

PUT UP A NESTING BOX

Three things determine the type of bird your box will attract: the entrance hole size and shape, the size of the box, and the location of the box. Check your local extension publications or consult your state's department of fish and wildlife for charts matching these parameters with the bird species you want to help out.

As an example, the American kestrel requires a 3-inch opening, 1 to 12 inches above the floor of the box. The floor dimensions should be 8 by 8 inches or 9 by 9 inches. Sawdust 2 or 3 inches deep should be put in the bottom of the box. The total height of the box should be 14 to 16 inches and the box should be 10 to 30 feet above the ground. The box should be put out between March and May in orchards or on the edges of relatively open areas. The opening should face west or south, and the boxes should be at least a half mile apart.

Place your nesting box near food, water, and/or escape cover. Predator guards might be necessary to keep out raccoons and cats. If your box is being used by a seasonal nester, clean out the box after the fledglings are gone; this will reduce parasite infections and make the box less attractive to mice.

One way to get ideas for the kind of structural diversity you might provide in your naturescape is to visit nearby natural areas when the birds and mammals are most active, usually sunrise or sunset/early evening. Stand still, look up, lift some rocks, move the underbrush aside, gently dig into the duff and the soil, and see what kind of life you find. Then think creatively about how to imitate nature's design. For instance, a wildlife biologist I know likes to have salamanders and newts in his yard, since they are voracious insectivores. To provide the warm, protected habitat they need, he simply lays a metal garbage can lid on the ground; the edge where the metal touches the earth simulates a rock's crevices to the amphibians. They find this new habitat and crawl underneath the lid within a few days.

Your naturescape can similarly provide habitat by supplying edges. Edges are where one type of ecosystem abruptly gives way to another. In what is known as the edge effect, most plant, insect, and animal (including human) life is found here.

Edges are everywhere in nature. One example is the edges of ponds. Plants grow in abundance, their roots enjoying the ample groundwater and dynamic seasonal flooding. Small mammals hide among these plants, living off the abundance of insects and plant life. Birds of prey nest high above them, enjoying the profusion of small animals. Larger animals come out of the deep woods on occasion to feast on the ample nutrition as well, both flora and fauna.

Natural edges are full of wildlife, but man-made edges can be, too. Zoologist Eugene Odum noted in 1971 that the density of songbirds is greater on estates and campuses and in similar settings than in tracts of uniform forest.

Nesting boxes are a great way to attract birds to your naturescape. This box, set among giant delphiniums, is a welcoming site for chickadees, wrens, and swallows. Design by Kim Hawks.

This screech owl found a perfect sunning spot in the hollow formed when a limb broke off an old apple tree in a Connecticut front yard.

This man-made rock pile has all the components of a happy reptile habitat: large rocks that predators can't move, southern exposure for warm sunning, and lots of holes for easy hiding.

This fawn has found shelter on the woodsy edge of a large meadow.

Whether you live in the city, suburbs, or country, your naturescape can create an edge. City gardeners will find that their naturescaped yards contrast with hard structures and pavement. Suburban naturescapers might find that although there might be a lot of greenery in their neighborhoods, there are not many native plants; their gardens will provide that needed native-plant oasis (which is all edge). Rural naturescapes will contrast with the surrounding monoculture of traditionally farmed megafields or the relative monoculture of meadows and forests.

If you build it, they will come. I am always amazed at how fast frogs find a newly built pond in the summer. I have a friend who simply dug a huge hole and filled it up with her garden hose. Within a few weeks the frogs' enthusiastic mating calls had her closing her windows at night to get some sleep. There are scouting parties in your yard right now, searching for that perfect snag to perch on or rock to crawl under.

Access to similar ecosystems nearby (space)

To thrive and breed without inbreeding, many of our wildlife populations need space: uninterrupted nature. Turf wars abound in the animal world, because mama needs her space. In many cases, the female will shoo off the male once his husbandly duties have been performed. And once the offspring are capable of leaving, they are encouraged to move along, too.

Most wildlife populations need to move around, and not just linearly. They need to move like kids in a playground, like fireworks in the sky—a bunch here, a burst there. With our naturescapes we do what we can, but there's only so much space a yard can provide. We need to try to create safe passage between our yard and other like environments: wildlife corridors.

If you live in the city or suburbs, talk to your friends and neighbors (and that includes nearby schools, parks, and churches) and get them interested in creating their own naturescapes. Together, your yards could be a working wildlife corridor, especially if you add native shrubs along every fence—or instead of fences (nature abhors a property line). A city (or suburb) block does not a corridor make, however; you might need "newt crossing" signs and such. But many of our newer neighborhoods are cul-de-sac rich, which can allow for plenty of uninterrupted land. Perhaps a map of your neighborhood might give you ideas.

If you are naturescaping in a rural area, hedgerows may be your solution. Hedgerows, also known as conservation buffers, are continuous plantings of a variety of (usually) native trees and shrubs. There is no set formula for the width of a hedgerow, but they are usually 5 to 20 feet wide. Because they host so many species of insects and birds, they are often incorporated into the pest management strategies of organic farmers (and traditional farmers who are realizing that their synthetic pesticides are getting more expensive and less effective as the years go on).

Hedgerows can host everything from ants to wolves. The Xerces Society (named after an extinct butterfly), a nonprofit organization promoting invertebrate conservation through research and education, is funding research into this new (old) idea. Many soil and water conservation districts are helping farmers and rural dwellers to create hedgerows; you can contact either group for good information on how to start your own. *Conservation Buffers: Design Guidelines for Buffers, Corridors, and Greenways*, a publication available online from the U.S. Department of Agriculture at http://www.bufferguidelines.net, is also an excellent resource.

Let Nature Do the Pest Patrol

A major reason for inviting every creature and his brother into your naturescape is that nature is the ultimate pesticide. It provides natural predators such as lacewings and ladybugs to keep aphids in check, as well as nematodes and hungry birds to control slugs. By including diverse plantings and the conditions to attract beneficials in your naturescape design, you can encourage a healthy balance between predators and prey. If you were to instead plant a monoculture of nonnative species and use insecticides, you would create the ideal conditions for a pest outbreak. Too many gardeners unwittingly set themselves up in that way for an endless war with nature.

The trouble with pesticides—and integrated pest management

Homeowners apply more pesticides per acre than do commercial agricultural operations. The herbicides we use on our lawns, as well as the insecticides we spray on our roses leach into groundwater and run off into storm drains. They eventually end up in rivers and oceans, where they diminish the health of fish and birds. For example, the insecticide diazinon has been shown to disrupt the behavior of Atlantic and Chinook salmon.

How did we get to this point? Immediately following World War II, a large percentage of the U.S. population moved to the suburbs. Pesticide companies convinced these first-time landowners that they should treat their tiny plots of land as miniature farms. That is, they should plant disease-prone, alien plants and monoculture lawns, and if a disease or pest arrived, they should treat it with synthetic chemicals. But what eventually became apparent is that these solutions simply caused new problems: the pests got stronger, viable ecosystems died, and people started contracting cancers like never before. Farmers and gardeners alike wanted something new.

Enter integrated pest management (IPM). IPM gained popularity in the 1960s as a way for farmers and gardeners to avoid using the harsher synthetic pesticides, which were losing ground because pests were becoming resistant and people were reading Rachel Carson's 1962 best seller *Silent Spring*. With the help of agronomists and soil and water conservation agencies, farmers and gardeners learned to attack their pests with a wide arsenal of biological controls, from learning the perfect time in a pest's life cycle to attack to applying natural (but not less lethal) insecticides such as rotenone. With IPM, synthetic pesticides can be used, but only as a last resort.

While this more commonsense approach has the net effect of fewer synthetic pesticides going into our soils and waterways, it is another have-it-all solution, a variation on the status quo. It is still about creating susceptible monocultures and protecting them with pesticides (even though natural). IPM is a variation on a theme; we need a new song.

WORKSHEET 5: PLAN TO WELCOME WILDLIFE

How will you provide a water source that is clean and accessible? Jot some ideas for water features that will run and splash.

How will you provide a diverse and abundant food supply? List some natives you can plant that will feed butterflies, birds, and bees.

How will you provide structural diversity and edges? List some places where birds can nest and small creatures can take cover.

How will you provide access to naturescapes and/or natural areas nearby? Note the names of people you can talk to about creating corridors between your lots, or the names of plants you might use to create a hedgerow if you have that kind of room.

How to encourage a healthy balance

In *Bringing Nature Home*, Douglas Tallamy relates how during the first year in his new home, a neighbor's horse barn was producing houseflies by the millions, all of which seemed to venture into the Tallamy home. Without resorting to man-made insecticides, entomologist Tallamy reduced the fly population in his house to zero by adding native plants and nesting boxes to his yard. The plants provide hiding places for salticid spiders and the nesting boxes provide shelter for sparrows, both voracious fly predators. (The native plants also provide habitat for food sources for the spiders when flies are not plentiful.) Tallamy also allows leaves to remain where they fall in his garden, thereby providing moist overwintering sites for the predatory spiders that would otherwise die from desiccation.

Nature itself is more than competent to look after the health of your garden. If you incorporate diverse plantings, welcome beneficial insects, and relax while you let nature's predator-prey relationships work things out, nature's awesome powers will keep everything copacetic.

This anise swallowtail butterfly caterpillar eating its way through meadow rue in an organic garden is a tasty morsel for a passing bird. Because the garden is organic, the bird won't get a dose of pesticide from eating the critter and will live to do more pest patrolling. Chanticleer Garden.

Plant for diversity. A monoculture attracts pests and disease much more than if those same plants had been spread out among other plants. A mixture of evergreen and deciduous trees and shrubs, perennials and vines blooming at different times, annuals that come and go, ferns, grasses, and bulbs is confusing to bugs looking for a promising place to land and chew.

Welcome beneficials. Beneficials kill the insects you don't want in your garden. A proactive way to attract beneficials is to plant nectar-producing plants in your naturescape. Most beneficial insects love nectar—some even rely on it for a stage in their life cycle—so the nectar is a way to keep them in your garden even if a pest is not present at the moment. Some nectaries have beautiful flowers and others have more of that wild-meadow look; some, like dandelions, are even considered weeds.

Keep a relaxed attitude. It may feel difficult to sit back and relax when aphids are mobbing your native roses or spit bugs have taken over your strawberry patch, but you must realize that an abundance of a single species is just a temporary condition, probably gone by next year. So sit back and enjoy the birdsong.

PLANTS THAT ATTRACT BENEFICIAL INSECTS

FLOWERING SHRUBS

camellia

gardenia

rose

FLOWERING PERENNIALS AND ANNUALS

amaranth

black-eyed Susan

clover

coneflower

daisy

lavender

marigold

Queen Anne's lace

tansy

thistle

EDIBLES OR HERBS

anise

borage

calendula

caraway

coriander

dandelion

dill

fennel

sage

sunflower

sweet pea

thyme

FEED THE GOOD GUYS

Here are some of the beneficial insects you might want to invite into your naturescape, and how to attract them.

❧ **Lacewings** destroy soft-bodied insects of all kinds: aphids, mealybugs, some scales, thrips, mites, moth eggs, and small caterpillars. They can be purchased. They like nectar and pollen plants such as dandelion, goldenrod, corn, and angelica.

❧ **Ground beetles** eat snails, slugs, maggots, cutworms, and tree insects such as gypsy moths and tent caterpillars. Collect them from rotting trees and put them on some rotting logs or wood in your naturescape.

❧ **Ladybugs** (also known as lady beetles) eat aphids. Don't use pesticides, and encourage your neighbors not to either, and they will increase in numbers along with their food source (aphids).

❧ **Tachnid flies** attack cutworms, armyworms, tent caterpillars, cabbage loopers, gypsy moths, Japanese beetles, May beetles, squash beetles, green stinkbugs, and sow bugs. They are attracted to pollen and nectar flowers including dill, wild carrot, sweet clover, amaranth, goldenrod, and various herbs.

❧ **Trichogramma wasps** prey on more than 200 species of moths, including spring budworms, tomato hornworms, corn borers, and codling moths. You can encourage them by planting caraway, dill, anise, and clover. They can be purchased.

❧ **Fireflies** kill slugs, snails, cutworms, and other insect larvae. They thrive in long grasses without any pesticides or in moist leaf litter. They also like ponds and streams.

❧ **Dragonflies** and damselflies eat mosquitoes, flies, and midges. Encourage them by providing a water source with aquatic plants and don't clean the bottom of the pond. They like branches protruding out of the water or floating wood. Some larvae survive only if the water is well aerated, such as in a creek.

❧ **Big-eyed bugs** and minute pirate bugs eat thrips, mites, aphids, small caterpillars, and many other pests. You can purchase them and release them into your garden. Even if they don't find any bad guys, they will stay and eat pollen until they do.

Discourage Problem Animals

While you want your naturescape to be hospitable to most wildlife, there are some animals—such as rabbits, deer, gophers, moles, voles, raccoons, skunks, and even moose—that can cause real damage by eating shoots and leaves, stripping bark, and tunneling or digging holes that disturb roots. These unchecked populations no longer have their natural predators around, for one reason or another, so they upset the natural balance. Natural ways to deal with these pests include thinking like nature, making your yard inhospitable to them, using barrier methods, and finding a way to live with them.

Let nature be your guide

Try thinking like nature. To do this, you might need to do some careful observation again. For example, let's say a raccoon is eating the fish in your pond, which is bad because the fish are your natural mosquito eaters. Sit by a natural pond and you will realize that there are deep parts of the pond, places where the fish can hide from marauding raccoons. Your solution is to make sure your pond has some deeper areas.

The inhospitable yard

To make your yard inhospitable, take away the problem animal's food and habitat and invite its natural predator (or something that mimics it) in. There is nothing that says your yard must provide water, food, shelter, or space for an out-of-control population; in fact, by doing so you are contributing to that problem. Think first about planting things that problem animals will avoid, then about creative measures you might take to scare away unwanted visitors.

Deer and rabbits seem to dislike chewing on hairy, waxy, bitter, and spiky plants such as acanthus, barberry, viburnum, forsythia, and skimmia, but you may have to do some experimenting to find out what the critters in your area shy away from. Your local cooperative extension may have a list; more general lists you might find in books or online can also give you ideas but may not peg exactly what works where you live. There are also disgusting formulations, both commercial and homemade, containing ingredients like cayenne, urine, and egg yolks, that you can spray on plants in the hopes of making them unpalatable to the pest that usually finds them delicious.

To discourage deer, you can try installing a sound scarer that turns on an FM radio and a bright LED light when activated by a motion sensor. And then there is the Japanese "deer scarer," a clever water feature that periodically makes a clanging sound as a bamboo pipe fills up; this is more of a pleasant than a scary sound, though, so I doubt many deer would notice this, much less be scared. Traditional scarecrows and their newer version, Mylar strips fluttering from wires strung around tempting crops, are scare tactics that sometimes work to keep birds away. For animals that burrow underground, there are solar-powered vibrating devices available that emit a deep vibrating noise at a pitch inaudible to humans and seem to trick moles into thinking there is another mole in the area.

A well-trained dog can be pretty good at keeping out unwanted visitors, but it takes the right dog demeanor and a lot of training. And then there's predator urine; both natural and synthetic kinds are available on the market. The theory is that wild animals mark their territory with urine, and animals lower in the food chain stay away from marked areas to avoid becoming dinner. It might be worth trying in your naturescape, though most homeowners who have tried it say it doesn't work for deer.

Barrier methods

The third solution is to exclude the pest with some kind of barrier if the other methods don't work. By excluding the predator you are limiting its resources and diminishing its space. Reduced resources and habitat tends to inhibit rampant reproduction, which is good for the entire ecosystem.

Fencing is the most common way to exclude the bigger predators, especially deer. The fence has to be high (8 feet is ideal) and fairly substantial, since deer can jump even a 5-foot fence and can flatten a fence by leaning on it. Some homeowners even put a moat around the fence for good measure. Electrical wiring has been used for large acreages. Underground perimeter fencing, about two feet below ground, helps keep out the pesky diggers (but, then again, you have to ask yourself if this is really something you want to do; these animals eat a large number of grubs and insects while also aerating your soil for better plant growth).

Other forms of exclusion include putting a fine wire mesh just under the water's surface to keep out fish eaters out of ponds, and draping fruit trees and bushes with plastic mesh to keep birds from raiding the pantry.

Live and let live

And then there is the laissez-faire approach—deciding that these visitors don't bother you at all, or that you don't really need that plant that they love to destroy. This is my favorite solution, but I don't live where you live (literally and figuratively). Still, it's something that might just cross your mind if you find yourself seriously considering paying money for predator urine.

CHAPTER 4 HOMEWORK:
ATTRACT BIRDS, SMALL ANIMALS, AND BENEFICIAL INSECTS

☐ Complete worksheet 5, "My Plan to Welcome Wildlife."

☐ Think about spreading the word about naturescaping to your neighbors if you live in the city or suburbs; think about hedgerows if you are in a rural area.

☐ Plan to attract beneficial insects with diverse plantings.

☐ If problem animals become frequent visitors, either think like nature, make your naturescape inhospitable to them, use barrier methods to keep them out, or learn to live with them.

This electric deer fence around a garden in Connecticut slopes outward to confuse deer's depth perception. Electric wire is more economical if employed in very long stretches of fence. Design by Sydney Eddison.

Netting can be used to discourage birds from plucking fruit off trees and berry bushes. Design by Marny Smith.

chapter five

CHOOSE SUSTAINABLE MATERIALS

Choose materials that are environmentally sustainable for the built elements of your garden.

It's time to think about the ecological impact of your material choices, now that you have lots of ideas about plant choices and ways to attract beneficial wildlife but you haven't put your naturescape design on paper yet. The choices you make about materials for your hardscape (the structural, usually nonliving, elements of the landscape) have an impact on this world, for better or for worse. It takes an awareness of the consequences of your decisions as well as a willingness to go beyond the norm (that is, traditional landscaping materials) to make earth-wise choices. This chapter will give you that awareness and introduce you to some imaginative and resourceful alternatives to the norm. It will guide you through making a list of the materials you plan to use.

Think Before You Buy

To be conscientious about landscape materials, first you must be conscious. Question everything about traditional landscape materials, the things that you can purchase at your garden center, your local big-box store's gardening department, your lumberyard, even your stoneyard. Because, as with a lot of current landscape practices, the status quo is damaging our earth.

What follows are the things to think about before you buy something new. These are guidelines, not scriptures; thought provokers, not hard-and-fast rules. Your best bet is to consider the full range of options, throw out what doesn't work for you, and weigh the rest. Making conscious choices—rather than buying what the commercials tell us to buy—is the best we can do.

To purchase or not to purchase

Do you really need to buy it? Or can you beg, borrow, or share it? Perhaps you could rethink purchasing that fancy play structure—after all, all the kids in the neighborhood need only one. Maybe you could have the trampoline in your yard and someone else could have the swing set. Does every home need a patio set big enough for parties? What if all the neighbors chipped in for an extra patio set that anyone could borrow? Rethinking our natural tendency as Americans to be independent might lead to some good neighborly relations (or at least you might meet the neighbors).

Indigenous, ingenious

If you decide you need it, you can still stretch your thinking process to go beyond the standard materials. Think back to the time when folks could not go out and buy prefabricated landscape materials and install them in a weekend, yet still wanted walls and fences, an overhead structure, a nice place to sit, even pools and fountains. What did they do?

They used what was at hand. Boards, yes, but also branches, grasses, bamboo canes, straw, dried manure, crushed rock, chalk dust, hide, hair, and hay. Twigs were soaked to make them pliable and then bent and tied or glued into trellises, arbors, and furniture. Thin branches were woven between stakes to make fences or daubed with gypsum to make durable walls. Bamboo canes were used for fences as well as paving and ornamentation. Mud and straw were combined to make bricks and roof tiles. Stains were created from berries and vegetable extracts. Structures were weatherproofed with gypsum, mud, and/or straw. Stone was broken and carried to make paving, walls, and water features that stand centuries after being built.

To find out what techniques were used in your region, you may have to do some sleuthing. Your local historical museum would be a good place to start; it may have information on how local people lived before industrialization, what materials were abundant, and how they were used. Another source of ideas is to look toward ancient (or just preindustrial) cultures with similar climates to yours: if you live in the coastal Northeast, you could borrow ideas from England and Japan; in the arid West, you could look toward the Middle East and North Africa, and so on. Researching the old ways of making paths, fences, walls, and overhead structures around the world might inspire you to start an entirely "new" way of hardscaping in your area—one that is gentle on the land as well as your wallet.

BEFORE YOU PULL OUT YOUR WALLET

- Ask if you really need to buy it.
- Find out what others before you or in other parts of the world have used for the purpose you have in mind.
- Ask around for sources of free raw materials, often by-products from farms or factories.
- Repurpose discarded items.
- Consider how easy it will be to recycle or reuse a product.

Plant supports in this garden of vegetables mixed with companion ornamentals were made by the homeowner from pliable twigs and small branches harvested during the annual winter pruning of trees on another part of the land. Design by Thyrza Whittemore.

This fence was built using scrap lumber and branches cut from juniper trees on the property. It serves the purpose of creating a boundary between a densely planted area of the garden and a more open, casual area, and it adds texture and local character to the scene. Design by Betsy Arriola.

Look to what has been used in the past where you live, or in similar climates, for inspiration. In this Southwest garden, the homeowner used a traditional medium, adobe, to make bricks and mortar. Design by Suzanne Derrer.

Is it a fence or is it art? Rebar topped with old bottles set at different heights makes an attractive boundary marker/focal point.

CONSIDER ADOBE OR COB

Adobe and cob are those old/new-again materials that just might work in your naturescape. Both can be used to make garden walls and benches as well as entire garden outbuildings.

Adobe is a natural for the Southwest: structures made of it keep the inside air cooler in the daytime and warmer at night, great for a place where the temperatures rise sharply and plunge daily. Adobe bricks are a mix of sand, clay soil, and straw. They are dried in the sun, then stacked with mud mortar. They are usually plastered with this mud as well.

Cob has been used in northern Europe for centuries, even in rainy and windy climates, to build house walls. It is made from hand-formed lumps of soil mixed with sand and straw. People who have built with cob love it because it can be formed into any organic shape. You can add a window wherever you please, or insert a niche, or decorate it with marbles and icons. Cob is enjoying a renaissance because it is an economical and empowering method of do-it-yourself construction. See http://cobworkshops.org for a listing of cob building workshops and events all over North and South America.

By-products, not products to buy

Thinking in terms of using materials at hand, particularly free materials that are the by-product of some form of local production, can save you a lot of money. Ask around. Find out what the local farms grow and what their by-products are. Here in Oregon we have hazelnut groves, and the cracked shells make a lovely path material that is long-lasting and that ties in visually with nearby trunks and branches; walking on this material generates a sharp crunch that is somehow restful. Similarly, Mount Vernon was lined with genteel white paths, a by-product of the Potomac River's oyster industry (in George Washington's time there were no restrictions on removing oyster shells). Farms are usually eager to give you by-products that are useless (or overwhelming) to them, but you will have to haul these gifts away yourself. With a borrowed truck and a batch of homemade cookies (for the farmers), you'd be surprised what you might glean—anything from aged manure to mint hay to used tools.

Don't forget local manufacturers. Asking friends what their company's (or department's) waste products are might get you thinking: maybe I can make a fence of that, or stack it into a wall, or lash it together to make a trellis. Shipping pallets, for instance, can easily be recycled into compost bins. Stone scrap left over from the manufacture of kitchen counters can be turned rough side up to serve as stepping-stones.

Another source of materials is our public lands. If you ask the appropriate local authority for permission, you might be surprised to find that you can help yourself to (a small amount of) an abundant natural resource, such as beach sand, river gravel or cobble, or fall leaves. Before asking for permission, be sure to have in mind what you want, how much you want, when you would like to remove it, and how you propose to haul it.

Reimagine and repurpose

Every culture since the dawn of time has used what is abundant to make shelter and landscape structures. Our twenty-first-century world also has some things in abundance. Sadly, our abundance can be found in our landfills, where we have discarded household goods that have outlived their usefulness or stylishness, or simply don't work anymore. Enter repurposing. Repurposing takes a usually discarded item, say an old door, and fixes it up so it can have a new life as something else, say a picnic table. It is seeing the potential. It's cleaning something up, sanding it, turning it upside down, cutting it up, epoxying it, attaching it to something else. It's painting it chocolate brown, lime green, or sparkly gold. It's giving old things new life.

BY-PRODUCTS THAT MAKE GOOD LANDSCAPE MATERIALS

cracked nutshells

crushed seashells

crushed pottery, tile, or brick

shredded or chopped tree bark (bark dust) or wood chips

wooden shipping pallets, wood scraps

scraps of rebar or steel plate

aluminum flashing and tubing scraps

scrap marble and granite

I've seen great repurposed items in gardens: an old desk fitted with a secondhand sink to make a handy potting bench with a built-in soil funnel; cut-off sneaker soles placed in a concrete path to look like footsteps; and even a string-and-yogurt-cup rain chain. This has no bounds! House salvage shops and secondhand stores are great places to start. Walk around these places with new eyes; don't see what it was but what it could be. And, above all, have fun with it.

One caveat, though: to avoid tackiness, the repurposed part should not be easily identifiable as its former self. The less it looks like its past life, the better. No old shoes planted with succulents, no brass bed filled with pansies—these have already been done. Better to make beautiful, useful garden pieces and elements that look vaguely familiar but can't quite be placed, like a movie title that is maddeningly on the tip of one's tongue. It will add a touch of intrigue to your yard, and humor as your visitors solve the riddle.

If you must buy new . . .

In some cases, buying new is your only alternative. Purchasing new can be guilt-free if you choose products that are nontoxic, have high recycled content, are locally produced, are durable, and are modular. It would be difficult to find one product with all of these attributes, but thinking in these terms will help you make informed decisions.

Toxic substances to avoid include paints and coatings with volatile organic compounds or VOCs, which contribute to smog and groundwater pollution. Also avoid arsenic and creosote, often used as wood preservatives in the past and found in old railroad ties, which have been sold as landscape timbers for many years. Stay away from any treated wood, and perhaps even rethink wood if it decays quickly where you live.

More and more new products have high recycled content. If you buy them, you will grease the recycling machine. Recycled content is high in some plastic landscape items such as rain barrels, composters, hoses, composite decking, and

GIVE OLD STUFF A NEW LIFE

Here are some ideas for turning salvage into hardscape. Use this list to jump-start your own creative musings about how to repurpose rather than purchase.

❧   Urbanite is an increasingly popular material for making steps, retaining walls, raised beds, and patios. It's simply broken-up concrete, repurposed. It's free and can usually be had for the asking if you see a pile of it at a construction site. You haul and it's yours.

❧   Wire can be used to string together cans, bottles, or found objects such as beads or keys from a secondhand store to create rain chains or partitions to divide outdoor rooms.

❧   Old toolboxes make intriguing planters.

❧   Old toilet tank lids can be painted and used as stepping-stones. Just be sure to put strips of nonskid tape across lengthwise to prevent slipping and sliding on a rainy day.

❧   Wire cages picked up at a home salvage or used-building-material store can be filled with objects like cut branches or glass bottles to create gabions, which can be used as tables or walls.

❧   Old sheets can be transformed into flags or canopies.

Old stuff can have a new life in your garden—and bring your garden to life. This rose-themed path makes creative use of old tiles and manhole covers gleaned from an urban renewal project in Portland, Oregon (the Rose City).

furniture. There is even recycled wood mulch, made from old pallets rather than virgin wood. If you don't see any of these products around, ask your retailer or write a letter to your local paper. Be the grease!

Taking a cue from locavores, who make a good effort to eat only locally grown food, you can make a good effort to purchase only locally manufactured landscape materials. You might find, as the locavores do, that this is harder than it sounds. But it can be done with a bit of sleuthing. Start at your garden center—ask where the item was made. If they can tell you it was made nearby, it's okay. If they don't know, ask for the name of the distributor, who can tell you where it was manufactured. You may find that the product is not made nearby at all, but by asking around you are raising retailers' awareness that this is important to consumers.

Decomposed granite mined nearby and local stone are attractive and durable hardscape materials. Design by Big Red Sun.

When given a choice, choose durable. For example, if you have decided on plastic lawn edging (to keep the grass roots from spreading to the adjacent flower beds), choose the more durable plastic. But also consider the bigger picture: what else can keep the roots at bay? Perhaps the answer is deep-set concrete blocks or natural stone.

And last, when buying new, chose modular over built-in. For example, if you want a patio, consider setting concrete blocks or natural stone in tamped sand rather than poured concrete (but do it accurately so it lasts for years without becoming uneven). That way, as the tides of landscape fashion change (they do, but slowly) you can give away, resell, or reset the pieces as you please—with no waste generated in the process.

The afterlife

Regardless of whether your landscape materials are shared, natural, by-products, repurposed, or new, there's one last (and lasting) thing to think about: what happens when they are no longer needed? Will they take a lot of energy to break up and remove? Will they fall apart, leaving an unsightly, even toxic, mess?

The best choice, in respect to the afterlife, are the biodegradable items. Nature knows what it is doing. Natural materials do not need to be removed; when they are done, they revert to their elements and regroup into something cool like food for a termite or mealybug. And rather than requiring energy to break down, they generate energy for the garden as they all but magically disappear. Espaliered trees, walkable ground cover, even cacti can make excellent hardscape stand-ins; we just need to expand our definition of hardscape.

PLANT YOUR HARDSCAPE

Webster's defines hardscapes as "structures that are incorporated into the landscape." Although hardscape is conventionally understood to be nonliving, there's no reason why plants can't serve as structures that are incorporated into the landscape. Here are a few ideas:

❧ For a security wall, try planting a hedge of cactus, barberry, pyracantha, or holly.

❧ For a fence, why not use a thin hedge of upright shrubs or trees like hornbeam or arborvitae, or a cordon (a freestanding tree or shrub that has been trained to grow flat)?

❧ For latticework, an espaliered tree or shrub (one trained to grow flat against a structure) will work just fine.

❧ For a patio, let an organic lawn or a walk-on ground cover be the pavement.

❧ Instead of building an arbor, plant a tree to provide shade and something for your clematis to twine on.

❧ For a play structure, make an easy way up into the lower branches of a mature tree by nailing wooden steps to the trunk, and be sure to put a very thick mulch underneath to cushion falls.

This apple-tree cordon at Mount Vernon is a freestanding fence that provides spring flowers and fall fruit. George Washington's Mount Vernon Estate and Gardens.

Trees make great living play structures (and also hammock supports), something many children have not forgotten.

Urbanite, or broken-up concrete, can be made into a rustic path, a low wall, or a raised bed for growing vegetables.

Another good choice in terms of its afterlife is a hardscape material that can be donated or sold to others when you are finished with it. If you are not sure if people will want it, you can peruse home salvage shops, want ads, or want-ad websites such as http://www.freecycle.org or http://www.craigslist.org to see what people give away or sell.

Know the Facts About Popular Materials

Some of our favorite landscape materials and features contribute to environmental degradation in ways most people are not aware of. For example, did you know that the piping commonly used in suburban irrigation systems is extremely toxic in its manufacture? Becoming aware of these damaging practices and of alternatives to popular materials will help you to decide which materials are right—or not right—for your naturescape.

Poured concrete

Concrete traditionally has three main components: Portland cement, aggregates (small rocks), and sand. Portland cement is a product of firing clay and limestone to 2700 degrees Fahrenheit. Besides requiring this staggering energy input, producing the cement releases lead, arsenic, and mercury into the air—and huge quantities of carbon dioxide. For every ton of cement produced, approximately one ton of carbon dioxide is released. Worldwide cement production accounts for 5 percent of global emissions of carbon dioxide, the main cause of global warming.

On the other hand, because concrete's heaviest component, water, is added onsite, transporting concrete produces less carbon dioxide from fossil fuels than do natural stone or concrete pavers. Also, concrete recaptures some carbon dioxide as it ages. And from a designer's standpoint, there are reasons to love poured concrete. It is extremely durable and can be a highly creative medium. It can be formed to any shape and it comes in lovely col-

ors that can complement the landscape (terra-cotta and near-black are my favorites). Interesting tiles, stones, or whatever (refrigerator alphabet letters?) can be added after the pour. The surface can be stenciled or stamped to bring a large expanse down to human scale.

For an earth-friendly variation on poured concrete, request a concrete mix with up to 50 percent fly ash (a by-product of coal production) instead of 100 percent Portland cement. Request that the aggregates be from crushed concrete rather than mined rock.

Good alternatives to poured concrete include tamped earth, tamped gravel, and decomposed granite, depending on where you live. Natural stone is always beautiful. Broken-up concrete reset in gravel (upside down or not) makes an interesting surface. Concrete driveways can be revitalized—and made permeable—by breaking up the concrete and re-laying it this way, too.

ALTERNATIVES TO CONCRETE

concrete mix with up to 50 percent fly ash and with crushed concrete as aggregate

tamped earth or gravel

decomposed granite

local, natural stone

urbanite (broken-up concrete)

Precast concrete pavers and wall blocks

Portland cement, a greenhouse gas contributor, is a key ingredient in concrete pavers and wall blocks. In addition, greenhouse gases are released in the transport of these heavy blocks. On the other hand, pavers laid over gravel can make a nice permeable driveway, parking area, or patio—and permeable paving doesn't harm your creeks and rivers and underground water. So should you use concrete pavers and blocks?

According to the Mid-Atlantic Precast Association, precast concrete can be made in a more earth-friendly fashion with industrial by-products such as fly ash and slag. Ask if your store's precast pavers or walls blocks are made with these recycled materials; if you don't find any, it wouldn't hurt to request them. If enough of us do that, we will eventually see change.

Instead of precast concrete pavers, you could consider the alternatives to poured concrete listed earlier. For concrete wall blocks, there are quite a few alternatives. You could use natural, local stone,

Natural, local stone is a durable and earth-friendly choice for walls and patios. This patio combines natural stone in various shapes and sizes with reused slate and brick and walk-on ground covers to create a permeable and attractive surface. Design by Plantscapes.

either dry laid or mortared in place. Walls like this have lasted for centuries. Locally produced brick might be a viable option—affordable as well as sustainable—depending on where you live The same goes for reused brick.

Hempcrete is a new material made primarily from hemp stalks and lime. It resembles concrete blocks but does not have the compressive strength of concrete. Its greatest asset is that it is carbon-negative; that is, the hemp production absorbs carbon dioxide, and even the bricks do, albeit very slowly. It might be something to consider if it is produced locally. There are also concrete-block alternatives such as large honeycombed blocks of clay, or compressed earth, but again, it only makes sense to use these materials if they are produced locally.

I would not recommend lumber as an alternative to wall blocks, however. To keep the wood from rotting, potentially toxic chemicals must be used to treat the wood and a waterproof membrane must be placed between the wall and the soil. Also, these walls are not extremely durable and need to be replaced in twenty or thirty years, which uses up more materials. And if the wood was soaked in preservatives, it is not suitable for many other uses and therefore most likely cannot be recycled or reused.

WHAT'S LEED GOT TO DO WITH IT?

LEED (Leadership in Energy and Environmental Design) is a green-building certification system that is internationally recognized and respected. Developers choose to build with the goal of achieving some level of LEED certification. Some governmental bodies are now demanding that new building and landscape construction meet LEED standards; others are offering incentives.

But how does LEED affect the conscientious consumer? As more and more developers are seeking certification, they are demanding products that help them achieve LEED points. For example, a builder will get one point for using materials with 10 percent recycled content and two points for 20 percent recycled content. So if a high-rise developer is trying to get LEED certification, you can bet that she will be looking to make a big purchase of concrete pavers with 20 percent recycled content. A concrete paver manufacturer who loses business due to lack of recycled content will quickly change the product line. And that's exactly what is happening. We are seeing more and more LEED-compliant building and landscaping products on the store shelves. In essence, LEED is making it a whole lot easier to naturescape.

Reused bricks are a good choice for a naturescape pathway because they hint of the area's history and save resources.
Design by Betsy Arriola.

Brick

Bricks are a popular choice for garden paths and walls because they are sized to be easy to work with, they are durable and strong, and they can be made locally around the globe. But firing the bricks in kilns requires huge amounts of energy, as does transporting them if they are not locally produced. And bricks need mortar to adhere them together in a wall, so this means using cement unless lime mortar is used.

The most sustainable choice is to use reclaimed bricks that are sourced locally. For patios and terraces, they can be set in a base of sand at least an inch deep to keep weeds from growing in the joints. Or you can set the bricks directly in the soil and add tiny succulents, herbs, or mosses in the gaps to keep out weeds.

For walls, you can mortar the bricks over a concrete base (there's no way of getting around this) using lime mortar rather than stucco. Lime mortar is simply water, sharp sand, and hydrated lime and contains no cement (stucco does). Using lime mortar will allow the bricks to be reused again in the future. Lime mortars are not as strong or durable as stucco mortars, however, so you might want to check with a local mason to find a lime mortar mix that will hold up in your climate.

Make sure if you use reclaimed brick that the brick has been fired especially for outdoor use and isn't from interior house walls. The latter isn't as hard and will start to flake and chip; a hard frost will turn indoor-type brick to dust.

Asphalt

Asphalt—also known as blacktop, tarmac, or AC (for asphaltic concrete although there is no concrete in it)—is not exactly a green product, but neither is it the worst choice. It is 100-percent recyclable and can even be removed and re-layed completely on-site. This is usually done with larger pavement projects; for driveways, the old asphalt is normally broken up and trucked away for recycling, and new asphalt—sometimes made with recycled content—is brought in.

Asphalt is made of crushed gravel and sand bound together with a by-product of crude oil refinement. It must be laid hot, and of course big trucks are needed to carry the raw materials to the site and also extrude the asphalt. A newer kind of asphalt, called warm-mix asphalt, requires less heat when it is laid and is considered a greener alternative. The product is just as durable and strong as the hot-mix asphalt. For a short driveway that gets very little traffic, you may even consider the cold-mix alternative, which is usually recommended for service roads because it is not as durable as the other types.

The jury's out on whether using asphalt as a driveway (and/or path) material is good or bad for the environment. On one hand, it uses fossil fuels in its raw materials, transportation, and production. On the other hand, it is recyclable; a homeowner can choose the energy-saving warm-mix asphalt (or even the cold-mix); it is available in a permable form, which is good for our water sources; and it can be made in light tones so as not to contribute to the urban heat island effect of many of our cities and suburbs.

Wood

Wood wants to decay in the out-of-doors—that's a given. There are some woods that decay more slowly than others, but those are expensive and from faraway places. Often, homeowners choose inexpensive, less-resistant wood that has been treated with preservatives to resist decay. The problem is, these preservatives are sometimes harmful to humans (arsenic was a common ingredient in wood preservatives until December 2003) and can be tracked indoors, where they contribute to indoor pollution. Decks often need reapplications of stain and varnish to look good and avoid splintering.

Imported woods with incredible strength such as ipe (Brazilian walnut, pronounced ee-pay), mahogany, and teak are sometimes used for decks. They are often touted as sustainable because they are highly decay-resistant, but transportation and tropical forest degradation may put that sustainability equation a little out of balance.

For an earth-friendly variation, choose a decay-resistant wood that is grown locally and sustainably. Resistant woods that are endemic to your region are your best bet. In the United States, look for redwood, black walnut, cedar, black locust, eastern red cedar, juniper, and cypress. Leave the wood untreated, or use earth-friendly stains and sealers. Excavate soil and place boulders or old concrete under the deck where it would otherwise come in contact with soil. If you can justify using ipe, mahogany, or teak, use wood certified by the Forest Stewardship Council.

As an alternative to wood, a combination of wood and plastic called composite can be used for decking, fencing, and retaining walls. You might like the idea that it is a product of recycled plastic and that no stains or preservatives are needed to keep it looking good, but some manufacturers allow shredded PVC in the product. PVC is not recyclable in most places so you may end up with no choice but to dump your old decking into the landfill. Instead, buy PVC-free composite decking and make sure it is recyclable where you live.

Decking tiles are a relatively new alternative to traditional wood decking. The tiles, which measure about a foot square and are made from cut natural stone or composite, are placed over a metal grid.

LANDSCAPE LIFESPANS OF NATURALLY DURABLE WOOD
(FOR HEARTWOOD THAT IS NOT IN DIRECT CONTACT WITH STANDING WATER)

eastern red cedar: 30+ years

redwood: 10 to 30 years

western red cedar: 10 to 25 years

white oak, bur oak: 10 to 15 years

Polyvinyl chloride (PVC) pipes

PVC pipes are a durable material for irrigation systems, but Greenpeace asserts that the production and incineration of PVC releases dioxin and "other highly toxic and persistent contaminants" into the environment. Also, PVC pipe is not recyclable.

An earth-friendly variation on PVC pipe is high-density polyethylene (HDPE) irrigation pipe, which is nontoxic and recyclable. As of this printing, HDPE pipe costs a bit more than PVC pipe because it does not have the same integrity and the walls must be thicker. However, the thicker walls are less susceptible to damage.

A better naturescaping solution is to avoid the need to use irrigation pipe altogether by choosing and locating your plants so that they need no watering once established, and by not watering your lawn—or reducing its size so that you can comfortably water it by hand or with portable sprinklers.

LOOK FOR FSC-CERTIFIED WOOD

The Forest Stewardship Council (FSC) is an international nonprofit organization that rates wood products based on responsible harvesting, fair trade, and cultural sensitivity. Founded in 1993, this is a legitimate organization that has improved forestry practices around the world. (Don't be confused by other acronym-certifiers; they are often bogus products of the timber industry.) FSC-certified wood has met strict standards, and the rating system is, as the FSC puts it, "the world's strongest system for guiding forest management toward responsible outcomes."

FSC-certified wood is becoming more and more available. If you do not see it at your retailer, ask for it; it's probably there or can be special-ordered. If they don't carry it, go to the store in town that does. In most cases, FSC-certified wood is no more expensive than comparable uncertified wood.

All wood certified by the Forest Stewardship Council sports the FSC logo.

In-ground landscape lighting

Light pollution is a result of outdoor lights that illuminate much more than is needed or even desired. It is created by those annoying fixtures that allow glare to go out and upward instead of where it is intended—usually downward.

Light pollution is becoming a very real problem for wild animals. Nocturnal animals such as bats, raccoons, coyotes, deer, and moose have difficulty foraging for food when their vision is impaired by bright lights. Some of these populations have experienced increased mortality because they rely on their night vision for collecting food and seeing predators. Night-flying migrating birds even wander off course, and do not reach their natural destinations, as a result of light pollution. Moths and other insects fly around the fixtures, wasting their limited energy reserves, leaving no energy for mating or migration. This, of course, diminishes their populations—and that of the animals that rely on them for food and the plants that need them for pollination.

For these reasons, you may choose to forego built-in landscape lighting completely. Consider whether you will truly be spending time out-of-doors when it is dark (or will it be too chilly or muggy?) and how much light you really need to enjoy the evening. Perhaps candles, a single kerosene lamp, or a string or two of Christmas lights would do the trick. After all, to enjoy the garden at night is to enjoy the low-light ambience and the stars above.

Solar lighting, which seems like a slam-dunk naturescaping alternative at first glance, may not be such a great idea when analyzed closely. First, the manufacture and transport of these lights and all of their components add to your carbon footprint.

Usually made from plastic, with small solar collectors attached to the post, they are not recyclable. One more drawback: because they do not need to be attached to a power source, they are easy targets for thieves. In light of all this, do you really need them?

Of course, you may prefer to have some lighting for safety and security purposes. To light your yard without contributing to light pollution, make sure your fixtures toss the light downward only, and the eye never sees the lamp (bulb). Purchase light-emitting diode (LED) or compact fluorescent lighting (CFL) bulbs for outdoor lighting. Turn off the lights when you are not in the area or are not viewing the garden from inside the house (timers will help with this). For wildlife safety, use long-wavelength lights with a red or yellow tint. For security, use motion-detecting sensors rather than floodlights; sensors catch intruders in the act. Or don't light the area: studies have indicated that there is no conclusive correlation between residential night lighting and reduced crime.

Make Your Materials List

Now that you have the lowdown on popular but environmentally harmful landscape materials and their more earth-friendly alternatives, think about what you want to use in your naturescape for surfaces, boundaries, and other features. Begin by taking out the list of material preferences you started to make in chapter 1, along with any images of desirable hardscape materials you may have clipped for your naturescape file. Making a list should help clarify what is important to you in terms of sustainability and landscape materials.

This naturalistic lantern lights an entry path without shedding excessive illumination. Design by John McKay Blois.

WORKSHEET 6: **MATERIALS TO USE**

JOT DOWN YOUR IDEAS ABOUT MATERIALS TO USE FOR DIFFERENT HARDSCAPE ELEMENTS YOU PLAN TO INCLUDE. CHECK INTO LOCAL AVAILABILITY AND COST, AND MAKE NOTES ON THAT HERE TOO.

ENTRY PATH (TO FRONT DOOR):

PRIMARY PATHS AROUND THE YARD:

SECONDARY PATHS (THROUGH BEDS):

DRIVEWAY:

PARKING AREA:

PATIO OR TERRACE:

DECK:

STEP RISERS AND STEP TREADS:

WALLS:

FENCES AND GATES:

OTHER WAYS OF DIVIDING SPACES:

WATER SOURCE OR FEATURE:

ORNAMENTAL ITEMS:

LIGHT SOURCES:

IRRIGATION SYSTEM:

STAINS AND FINISHES:

OTHER:

Surfaces

It should be clear to you by now that your choice of surfaces—decks, patios, paths, steps, driveways, and parking areas—has an effect on our planet. These hardscape decisions also have a direct effect on the feel of your naturescape, your garden aesthetic. For example, brick paths evoke tradition and formality whereas roughly surfaced stones set in a free-flowing pattern suggest a rugged naturalism. Even different types of gravel give different messages: smooth gray-and-black gravel lends the garden a classic, sophisticated feel; rough gravel made from tan and sienna-colored volcanic rock gives a warm, casual feel.

In general, the smoother the surface—think glassy flagstone—the more formal the aesthetic. The rougher the surface—think volcanic rock or coral—the more naturalistic and casual. But you can play with these messages. Think of using cut flag (flagstone cut into rectilinear patterns) to make a meandering path of varying widths—the formal made into the informal. Or you could try the reverse: use casual, natural materials in a

This path of roughly surfaced stone set in soil with occasional brick banding evokes a rugged naturalism. Design by Belinda Kaye.

formalistic pattern, like edging a straight path with volcanic rocks.

Another aesthetic rule of thumb is that darker materials recede visually. So if you have a lot of something, say a wide path, you may want to use a black or dark gray gravel rather than a mix of tans and whites.

In terms of cost, choosing local materials will save you money, although you may be more limited in your choices. It's hard to generalize about prices of surfacing materials, because they can vary widely from place to place (based on distance from the raw sources, local price competition, the local building industry in general, and even natural disasters and world events), but what's plentiful and near at hand will cost less than what's scarce and exotic. You also need to factor in the labor costs, which are significant with stonework in particular, and delivery charges.

Chipper mulch makes a fine surface for paths in a naturescape. It's inexpensive or free, it's biodegradable (this homeowner refreshes hers every couple of years), and it looks natural. Design by Lorraine Anderson.

RELATIVE COST OF SURFACE MATERIALS, LEAST TO MOST EXPENSIVE

wood chips

gravel from crushed rock

gravel from river (smooth) rock

concrete, poured in place, do-it-yourself

concrete pavers

asphalt

wood decking

new brick

natural flagstone

used brick

Durability is also an important factor in your choice of surface materials. Although durability varies from region to region and even from backyard to backyard, here are the average lifespans, or how long it takes to look shabby, of common surface materials:

- Bark dust or wood chips (for paths): 1 to 5 years
- Sand and pebbles over a weed-barrier membrane (for paths): 3 to 10 years, if kept weed free
- Chemical-free heartwood (not touching anything moist): 3 to 30+ years
- Brick or tightly laid natural stepping-stones, set directly in soil: 5 to 10 years until they need to be reset, depending on frost heave and soil texture
- Bricks, concrete blocks, or natural stone set in mortar: 20 to 30 years until the mortar breaks down
- Bricks, concrete blocks, or natural stone set in sand: 50+ years, if kept weed free and sand is added periodically to keep the pavers tight
- Natural stone set directly in soil, as stepping-stones: infinity

Boundaries

Boundaries are the landscape elements that will define the different spaces of your naturescape. They can be built, such as walls or fences, or grown, such as hedges and cordons. Along with surfaces, your choice of boundary materials defines the aesthetic of your yard, so choose mindfully based on the feel you want, as well as sustainability, cost, and durability.

Fences can be made of boards, but they can also be made of sustainable wood substitutes such as bamboo and wattle. Bamboo is getting a lot of attention these days as a sustainable alternative to wood because it grows so quickly. A wattle fence is made by interlacing flexible twigs horizontally between upright poles, which are usually sturdier, straight branches, giving the effect of a basket-weave pattern. If you have access to a supply of bamboo canes or pliable willow or alder branches, using these materials for fencing would make good sense. Instructions on how to make these kinds of fences are available online and in books.

Walls can be stone, brick, concrete or concrete alternatives, adobe, cob, or any other material that holds up in your weather. Material strength is an important consideration here, particularly for retaining wall. In fact, if your retaining wall is going to be tall, you probably will need to have it designed by a civil engineer or architect; check your local building codes. A well-built wall can last longer than any other element in the garden, so consider that you might be building for future generations.

On the other end of the permanence spectrum is the hedge, plants used as space dividers. To avoid the need for fussy maintenance, use rows of tall shrubs rather than hedges that need shearing. You can espalier a row of trees or shrubs of the same type—that is, prune them so they are flat, creating a narrow, fencelike row. Grapevines and dwarf fruit trees can be pruned to make cordons, mentioned earlier. Informal hedgerows—thickets of trees and shrubs—will provide a haven for insects and animals while they are also defining separate areas of the garden.

Other features

Water features, art, lights, garden furniture, and structures like arbors and gazebos provide focal points—that is, they punctuate space with something that draws the eye—and add interest in the naturescape. All can be made of sustainable and/or local materials. This is where you can get really creative with repurposing and recycling.

For water features, think about ways to use seasonal rainwater to make your garden interesting even when it's wet and cold out. Sculptures and other artwork should be large enough to be in scale with plants in the garden. Use recycled materials, things from nature, or things from the house. Move art around until it feels good. Find old furniture

at thrift stores or used building material stores and apply indoor-outdoor paint for a shabby chic look, or look for new furniture made from recycled plastic.

Pergolas, arbors, gazebos—what's the difference? For the record, pergolas and arbors are small buildings that have beams overhead. They can be attached to a building or freestanding. Pergolas are a certain kind of arbor, usually a long arbor that covers a path. Gazebos, summerhouses, and pavilions are outdoor structures that are open on the sides and (usually) covered. Any of these structures can have vines growing up the sides and creating a roof if there isn't one already. Just remember: stay local with your materials as much as possible and be creative.

CHAPTER 5 HOMEWORK:
CHOOSE MATERIALS THAT ARE ENVIRONMENTALLY SUSTAINABLE

☐ When deciding on landscape materials, consider not buying, using old-fashioned methods, using by-products, or repurposing before buying something new.

☐ If purchasing new, try to go with products that are nontoxic, have high recycled content, are produced locally, and are durable.

☐ Where possible, avoid choosing materials such as PVC pipe that have a big environmental impact and instead choose less harmful alternatives.

☐ Complete worksheet 6, "Materials to Use."

chapter six

LOOKS GOOD
ON PAPER

Let nature be your guide as you put design decisions on paper.

You've carefully observed your yard, your region, and your own wants and needs. You've educated yourself about water issues, plant and material choices, and wildlife requirements. You've taken notes and assembled inspiring images. You've mapped your backyard biohabitats. With all this information in hand, you're ready to move to the next step: distilling what you've learned into a list of design goals and committing your design ideas to paper so that you have a plan to follow. In other words, you're going to design your naturescape.

The purpose of this chapter—which guides you in creating a functional diagram, a landscape plan, and a planting plan—is to help you make decisions that are best made before you put shovel to soil. You don't need to nail down every detail; in fact, many of your design decisions—like the routing of a dry creek or the placement of trees to give a grove effect—might best be made in the field, where nature can be your codesigner. But you will be encouraged to work out some of the more major aspects of your design, such as the choice of materials for a new patio, as well as its approximate shape, size, and location.

Throughout this step it will be important to remember that you are designing with nature. And, just like nature, you do not have to be house-plans accurate. The important thing is to gather all that you have learned and to put it on paper in one form or another; it can be as rough—or as precise—as you wish. You will come to a point in this chapter where you feel you have made all of the design decisions you need to make, and you are ready to go out and work in your yard. At that point, whether it's at the end of the chapter or somewhere in the middle, feel free to move to the next chapter and start the installation.

Formulate Design Goals

You need to know clearly what your goals are in order to create a functional, highly satisfying naturescape that will give you pleasure for years to come. Design goals are what you want your yard to do for you. "Create a relaxing space" or "create a welcoming habitat for native insects and fauna" are design goals. A new patio is not a goal; it's a way to reach a goal, such as "create a space to have a party."

Making a list of your design goals is a great way to get creative, because for every goal you can probably come up with more than one solution.

And once you have a few solutions, you can choose the best one—the one that costs less, is better for the environment, requires less work, looks more beautiful, is more durable, and perhaps serves multiple purposes. So, putting the gazebos, lawns, fire pits, and patios aside, let's talk about what you want your yard to do for you.

From worksheet to goal list

To start your goal list, refer to worksheet 1, "What I Want and Need." As an example, suppose you wrote (quoting from an actual client's questionnaire, with permission): "We thought it might be nice to have at least a small area right off the house for having coffee, reading, etc., and a larger area for a table." This could be translated into the goals (1) create an area near the house for us two to read and have coffee, and (2) create an area in the yard where we could serve dinner for six or more people.

A good trick to make a list of design goals (rather than solutions) is to write, "I would like my yard [or my design] to . . . " as in "I would like my yard to be a place where I can read a book in comfort." Avoid the temptation to add the words *via*, *by*, or *with*, as in "I would like to create more privacy in my yard by adding tall trees." Can you see the difference? Those last four words cut off any other ways of arriving at privacy.

Of course, you might have a case where there is really only one good, viable solution to your goal. For example, if your patio works just fine where it's currently located but it's a little too small when all the relatives come over, it's okay to write "enlarge the patio" as a goal (although you could also write, "create a space to entertain twenty people").

When you write down your goals, they do not have to be in any particular order, but it helps to assign each goal an A, B, or C priority.

This statue, tucked away at the back of the property, fulfills the design goal of making the yard seem larger (by adding depth). Design by Sue Lyn Thomas.

WORKSHEET 7: **DESIGN GOALS**

I WOULD LIKE MY YARD TO: PRIORITY

---	A B C
---	A B C
---	A B C
---	A B C
---	A B C
---	A B C
---	A B C
---	A B C
---	A B C
---	A B C
---	A B C
---	A B C
---	A B C
---	A B C
---	A B C
---	A B C
---	A B C
---	A B C

Following are the design goals I had for my own naturescape.

I WOULD LIKE MY YARD TO ...

- ❧ have workable soil
- ❧ include a space to grow edibles
- ❧ have a smaller lawn area
- ❧ provide more shade on the south side of house
- ❧ have a romantic, lush, old-world feel
- ❧ include an area to entertain about twenty people
- ❧ provide an easy transition from house to entertainment area
- ❧ be more dog friendly
- ❧ have a place in the front yard/entry area to read the newspaper on warm evenings
- ❧ provide a covered area for potting plants and tool storage
- ❧ offer interest throughout the seasons

From goal list to design

Getting from your goal list to an actual design involves taking the map of your property that you created in chapter 3 and using it as a basis to try out various design solutions on paper. Your biohabitats map is a visual guide to the design solutions nature is pointing you toward. When you notice on your map where it fries in the summer, where there's standing water when the snow melts, or where the soil is just too rocky to plant anything, you can start to think of the best ways—and where in your yard—to meet your design goals. Making a functional diagram will help with this.

The functional diagram shows all the activities and elements you would like to have in your yard. For example, if you know you want a restful place in the yard (your design goal), you may choose a shady spot away from neighborhood noises to put a bench or a small patch of lawn (ways to meet your design goal). Going through goal after goal, you will probably find a spot on your functional diagram for everything. You may need to massage the design

A desire for fragrance mentioned in your list of goals might be satisfied by a solution like planting some old-fashioned heliotrope.

Home-grown tomatoes will satisfy a design goal of growing edibles, while nature and a little ingenuity provide the staking.

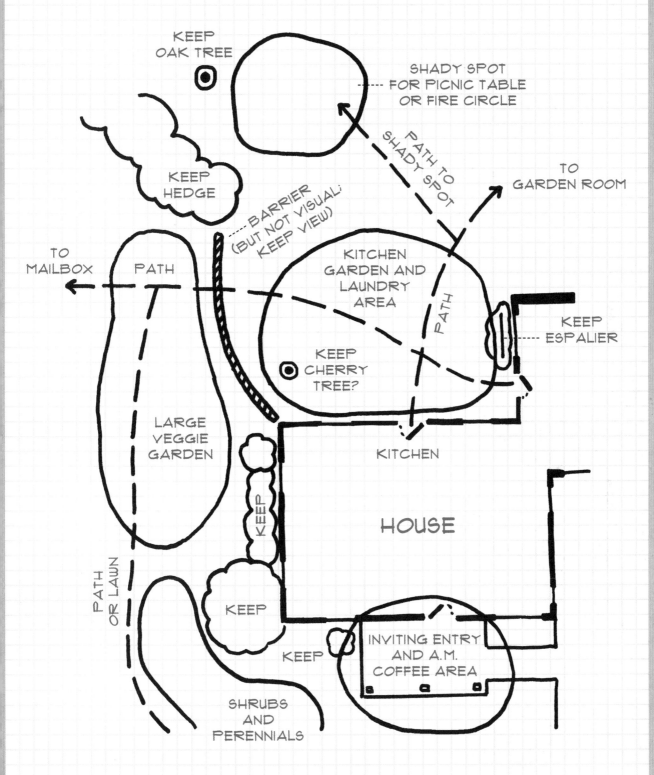

The functional diagram shows what features you want in your yard and roughly where they will be.
Check it over to make sure all your design goals have been satisfied.

a bit (move things around, make distinctive areas smaller or larger, put barriers between activities or, conversely, link them visually or actually). If your land offers you a choice of good locations for the elements you want to include, you'll be able to try different layouts on paper until you find the arrangement that looks just right to you.

To begin, tape a copy of the base map you created in chapter 3 to your drawing surface and get out the list of design goals (worksheet 7). Then tape a piece of tracing paper over your base map, get out your #2 pencil, and read over your goals. Have your biohabitats map near at hand; you may even want to tape this map to the wall next to your desk or work surface.

Starting with your A goals, figure out where each one can be satisfied on the map and draw a bubble around each area with a note about its use. For example, if a goal is "a serene place to do my yoga," circle the areas of your yard that are serene already—or that you can make serene with some kind of screening or barrier—and write "yoga?" Do this for each of your goals. Refer to your biohabitats map throughout this process; it will help you decide where to locate things.

As you are laying out these elements, make sure they are compatible with each other and massage the relationships where necessary. For instance, a patio might be great under your existing shade tree, but if that puts it right next to your new garbage and recycling center, moving things around a bit or creating a screen of some sort is in order. Because you will be going back and forth on decisions—this is the crux of the creative design process—your tracing paper may get hard to read or messy. When this happens, just overlay it with another sheet of tracing paper, copy the parts of the design that you like, then discard the original tracing paper.

When you have your elements placed, add dashed lines to indicate where you will want paths. Draw a striped line to indicate a barrier of some sort between adjacent areas. Continue working on tracing paper until all of your design goals have been satisfied (or rejected; that's okay, too). At this point, you will have made many design decisions

that will make it easy to draw your final landscape plan and your planting plan.

Draw the Landscape Plan

This is the point where all of the information you've gathered so far comes together into one drawing—the landscape plan. Although drawing up a landscape plan is not absolutely necessary to create a great naturescape—you might want to head out to the yard at this point with your functional diagram as your rough guide instead—it can be a very useful tool. The landscape plan shows everything that will be in your yard with exact dimensions. It will tell you if everything will fit and if the proportions are right. You will know ahead of time, on paper rather than after a hard day's work in the yard, if something just doesn't look right. You will be able to see if everything is in good proportion and if the shapes and curves you create are pleasing.

There are other good reasons to create a landscape plan. For one, it can help you avoid costly and time-wasting mistakes; for instance, if you know that eventually there will be an herb garden in a certain spot, you won't plant a tree there now (most herbs need sun). The landscape plan will also help you calculate the quantities of landscape materials you will need, such as mulch or lumber. The landscape plan is a great communication tool that you can use to get your family and friends (potential helpers!) enthused, to get your ideas approved by the local authorities, or to get a neighbor onboard. And, finally, it has archival value; if you decide—or need—to put off working on your naturescape, all of your thoughts, decisions, and research will not have been wasted.

Review materials and get a design on paper

To prepare for creating the landscape plan, look over everything you have gathered so far, all the worksheets you've completed along with images and ideas you've collected, so it's fresh in your mind. Take a copy of your base map and tape it to your work surface. Overlay it with your functional diagram, and, as before, have your biohabitats map nearby for easy reference. Tape a new sheet of tracing paper over your functional diagram.

Start by tracing over the things that will stay. Then draw in new hardscape elements such as an arbor, a patio, or a walkway. Anything that is not hardscape will be planting beds. Within these beds, add trees (just show the trunks) and the outlines of shrub masses and perennials showing the mature widths of the plants. If you have a certain kind of tree or shrub in mind, or just the height of a shrub mass, indicate it, but at this point in the design process it would only be distracting to choose every plant for each area, so avoid that temptation. For now, we are looking at the big picture. Don't forget that plants can have structural functions: a well-placed tree can block a poor view and a thick mass of native shrubs can beautifully separate two discordant functions.

Let the functional diagram under your tracing paper be your guide but don't feel limited by it. For example, you may have chosen a small sunny spot for your vegetable garden. But now you have decided to lay out the vegetable garden in a formal, radiating pattern, and the sunny spot you chose is not level enough for that. So you move the vegetable garden to another sunny spot that is level. Play around in this way, choosing different layouts and patterns, changing your tracing paper as needed.

Go outside

It may help, at a certain point, to go outside and pace off some of the spaces you are thinking of. You could even mark them with powdered chalk or field paint (used for marking playing fields; it eventually wears off) from the hardware store. Then go back to your drawing board and make adjustments.

A set of steps might make sense if your land slopes dramatically. Don't worry about nailing down the details on your landscape plan; let nature help you figure it out during installation.
Design by Karen Bussolini.

COMMON PATH AND WALKWAY DIMENSIONS

suburban sidewalk: 5 feet wide

entry walkway: 4 to 5 feet wide

path with steps: 4 feet wide

path for two people: at least 4 feet wide

path, comfortable single file: 3 feet wide

path, narrow single file (for access to plants through beds): 2 feet wide

stepping-stone path: each stone 12 to 16 inches wide, irregular

LANDSCAPE DESIGN TIPS

Follow these design tips to come up with an aesthetically pleasing naturescape:

Stay in scale. When working on your plan it is easy to start thinking that your land is larger than it is (perhaps because we are used to looking at maps, which cover a lot more land). A helpful way to keep in scale is to take the measurements of a piece of outdoor furniture you already have, like your patio table or chaise longue. Make a little cutout of it in scale with your drawing (if you're working off 1/8-inch gridded paper, this is 1 inch = 8 feet, or 1 inch on the drawing equals 8 feet in reality). Keep the cutout(s) on your drawing as you are designing.

Make meetings meaningful. Where one object meets another on your drawing, such as where a fence meets the house, have them meet at a "meaningful" spot, such as the house corner, or exactly between two windows, rather than at a random spot along the wall.

Make meetings right. When a curve meets a straight line on your drawing, such as when a curving lawn edge meets a sidewalk, have the two lines meet at a right angle. This avoids creating awkward pie-shaped planting spaces.

Mass your shrubs and perennials. Never call for a lone shrub or perennial; in nature they grow in masses. As a rule of thumb, you should make the width of the shrub mass at least double the mature height of the shrub. That is, if the shrub will get to be 3 feet tall, make your mass at least 6 feet in diameter, on average. For perennials your mass could be three times the height. Most designers like to mass in groups of three, five, seven, or more, creating naturalistic, amorphous shapes.

Repeat plants throughout the garden. Instead of using only one mass of a given shrub, repeat it elsewhere in the garden (or garden room). The mass could be a different size or shape, and it will probably be set against other plants; this will make your garden interesting, while the repetition will give the garden a sense of unity. The larger the garden, the more you will want to repeat plants.

Repeat plant elements. Choose a striking element—such as red foliage or spiky texture—and choose plants that share this characteristic. Scatter these plants (masses, not individuals) among the garden beds. This will also lend a sense of unity to your yard.

Choose contrasting colors. To make your garden pop, place contrasting colors (the opposite side of the color wheel, such as purple and yellow) next to each other.

Echo architectural details. Repeat some element of the house in the landscape to add cohesiveness. For example, if you are designing an arbor, you may want to repeat the house's windowpane height-to-width ratio in the arbor's latticework, or the angle of the house's roofline in the arbor's arch. These repetitions can be quite subtle; they do not have to be exact replicas of existing architectural features. The idea is to not introduce a new element when there are no other similar elements in sight. For example, don't make the top of your arbor curved when there are no curves or circles anywhere else on the house or in the landscape. However, if you will be having other curved elements in the yard, such as a round birdbath or a circular patio, this would be okay.

One of the secrets to a satisfying naturescape is to keep the landscape elements (lawn, patio) in scale with the home and yard size. Design by Big Red Sun.

Repeating elements, such as the diagonal bench slats that echo the roofline, help make this a harmonious view. Design by Dr. Gordon White.

It's a good idea to have the lines of your design meet at right angles, even if they are curving (left). Otherwise you will create awkward pie-shaped spaces (right).

If there is a slope to your land, you might want to consider meandering your paths or incorporating steps into your design. Decide roughly where the paths will go, then take a walk and let whatever is your natural route become the path. If the slope is steeper, the path will naturally meander more. If there is a spot where the land slopes dramatically, a set of steps might make the most sense.

Designing is a back-and-forth process. You will find that you zero in on a shape or feature that you really like, but you can't get the other parts right. So keep the good parts and on a new tracing paper overlay, try some wacky ideas for the parts that are not right. And remember, nature is forgiving. Beautiful, healthy plants make the best gardens; nobody ever notices if the beds are not the perfect size or the paths don't curve just so. Keep working at it, section by section, until you like the whole thing. This is your final design.

Make it pretty

You've made all of the decisions; now all that's left to do is to make it presentable. Take another sheet of tracing paper and place it over your final design. Draw everything on this sheet, including the entire house outline, with a #2 pencil. Add simple notes about landscape features, such as "compost bin," "gate with arbor," or "tire swing." Writing a little description near the feature—or with an arrow pointing to it—works better than a detailed explanation.

You may want to add color to make your drawing more understandable. You can use marking pens, but colored pencils are more economical and, if you make a mistake, easy to correct. Keep this original (because it is delicate) and make color copies to share your design with others and to take outdoors with you to refer to as you install your naturescape. You will probably want to keep one or two for archival purposes as well.

If you plan to mass potted flowers on one corner of the porch, the simple note "with pots" on your landscape plan will help clarify this. Design by Kent Greenhouse.

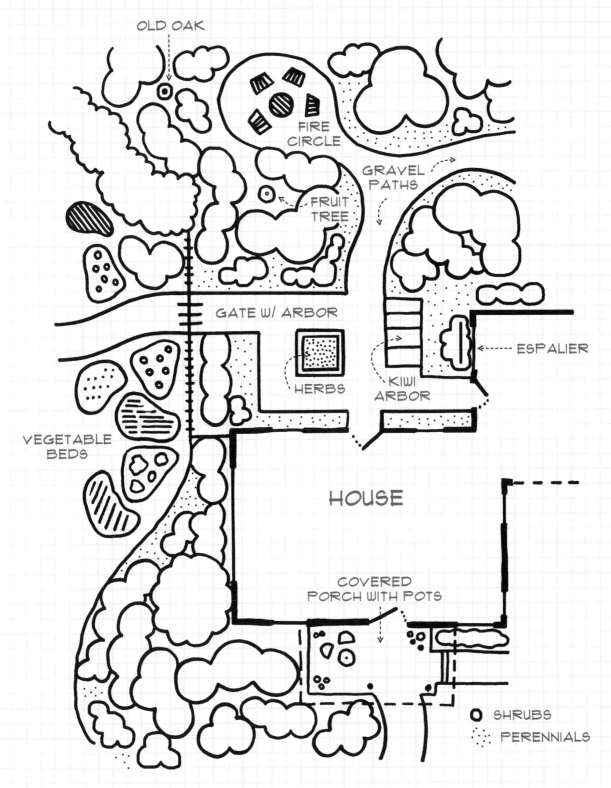

OLD OAK

FIRE CIRCLE

GRAVEL PATHS

FRUIT TREE

GATE W/ ARBOR

HERBS

KIWI ARBOR

ESPALIER

VEGETABLE BEDS

HOUSE

COVERED PORCH WITH POTS

O SHRUBS

⋮ PERENNIALS

Your landscape plan shows the new layout of the yard but does not get into the details of which plants to use. It should be understandable to others.

Landscape designers and architects use an array of construction drawings to convey a landscape design to those responsible for its installation: a layout plan, a grading-and-drainage plan, a site construction plan, a planting plan, and a sheet with detailed drawings of hardscape elements (such as arbors and gates) or how the trees should be planted.

Also included in the set might be an irrigation plan, a water-recycling (gray water) plan, and/or a lighting plan. You most likely won't need all of these drawings, but if you're more comfortable figuring out every last detail before you go outside with your landscape plan, you may want to make up a layout plan and sketch some details.

A layout plan is simply a copy of your landscape plan with a few exact measurements in relation to known items, such as your house, added in colored pen or pencil to stand out. Think forward to the day you are in your yard, ready to dig. What are the points that you need to mark on the ground in order to get everything laid out? Mark these points on your drawing and draw a line from each of them to an existing element, such as a house wall or baseline you have created. Measure the length, translate to the real-world distance, and write it down. You may want to add simple notes to this drawing as well, describing how you want something to look, how you want it installed, or referring to a photograph you have collected or a sketch you have (or will) make.

To sketch a construction detail, decide on the overall dimensions of the feature (for example, a gate-and-arbor might be 8 feet tall at its highest point and 5 feet wide). Choose a scale that will allow this drawing to fit onto an 8-1/2 x 11 sheet of paper with notes yet not be too small to view clearly. (If you choose a scale of 3/4 inch = 1 foot, the gate-and-arbor would be 6 inches tall and almost 4 inches wide on your drawing, which, with notes, would fit nicely).

Working in scale is a great way to make sure the dimensions are not off. Have you ever seen a tall arbor with spindly 4 x 4 posts that look like toothpicks? Sketching the detail will avoid this; you will see that it is funny looking on paper and can try using larger posts or having the posts rest on hip-high pillars. This is all a lot easier to fool with on paper than in the field. Another advantage of drawing up details is that you can price out each idea (which might help you decide which idea to go with).

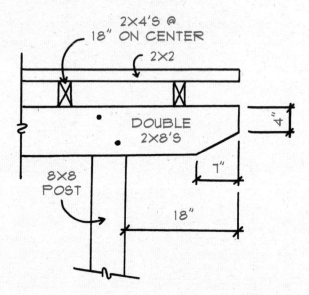

Details show how you, the designer, envision something like the top of an arbor will look. Drawing it to scale forces you to make the vision fit reality.

If you want a landscape element to look a certain way, you may need to sketch it out first. A scaled, detailed drawing of this gateway, consisting of two stone pillars and a metal arch, guided the contractor who built it. Design by Big Red Sun.

Make Your Planting Plan

A planting plan is simply a copy of your landscape plan labeled to show the details of every new tree, shrub, and perennial to be planted. Preparing a planting plan will help you figure out exactly how many plants of what type you need when you go to the nursery.

Start with a copy of your landscape plan. Take the backyard biohabitats chart (worksheet 3) and the preliminary plant list (worksheet 4) you prepared in chapter 3. For each bed, decide which biohabitat it is in, then look at that biohabitat's plant list. Start with the trees and largest shrubs, and work your way down through the perennials, ferns, grasses, and bulbs. For example, if your landscape plan calls for an 8-foot-tall evergreen shrub to separate two spaces, find a plant from your list that fits that description. If there isn't one like that on your list, you may need to do some research to find the right plant. A visit to the local nursery, a good native-plant book, or an online search will help you with this. You might need to go back and forth a bit in this stage of the design, from preliminary list to plan to book or website.

On your plan, show your plants as circles with a diameter that represents the eventual spread. The beauty of working from a scaled base map (rather than a rough sketch) is that you can figure out exactly how many plants you need and how far apart to plant them. By doing so, you won't end up ten years later with plants that are too close to the house or crowding each other out. Give each plant a different shorthand name (for example, "Vacc. ova." for *Vaccinium ovatum*) and indicate the number of plants in each grouping.

Design with plants

For the best effect, mass your plants in groups of three or five. Smaller plants can be in groups of five, seven, or more, and bulbs can be in even larger masses. With very large shrubs, you may need only one, or you may have a few placed throughout the garden, perhaps a group of three, one of two, and one alone. The point of massing is to create swirls of plants like nature does rather than having them scattered through the beds as if they were thrown like confetti. On your plan, show the masses as overlapping circles. For clarity, erase the inner lines and label the plants as a group, such as (5) Ascl. spec. (for *Asclepias speciosa*).

NARROW YOUR TREE AND SHRUB SELECTIONS ONLINE

The Arbor Day Foundation offers an online tool you can use to narrow your selection of trees and shrubs, the Tree Wizard at http://www.arborday.org/shopping/trees/treewizard/intro.cfm. You answer a few questions, starting with your zip code to determine your plant hardiness zone, and including your soil type, the sun exposure of the area you have in mind, and the eventual height and width of the ideal tree or shrub. With that input, a page appears showing the trees or shrubs that meet your criteria, with a photo of each and a link to full descriptions.

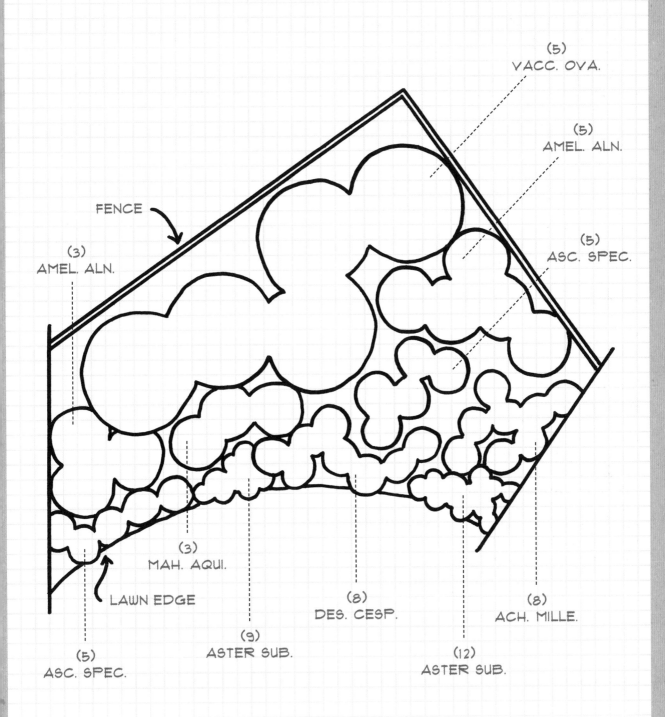

(5)
VACC. OVA.

(5)
AMEL. ALN.

(5)
ASC. SPEC.

FENCE

(3)
AMEL. ALN.

(3)
MAH. AQUI.

LAWN EDGE

(8)
DES. CESP.

(8)
ACH. MILLE.

(9)
ASTER SUB.

(12)
ASTER SUB.

(5)
ASC. SPEC.

*Show your plants on your planting plan as circles with a diameter that represents
the eventual spread. Give each plant a different shorthand name (Vacc. ova. = Vaccinium ovatum)
and indicate the number of plants in each grouping.*

To add interest, think about color and form as you place your plants. Place plants of contrasting textures against each other (spiky leaves next to large, rounded ones next to a plant with tiny leaves). Consider the colors of not only flowers and fruits but also foliage. Chartreuse leaves look great near purple flowers, for example. Playing with contrasting and complementary colors is another way of making an attractive garden. And remember to choose plants that will create interest in each of the seasons.

The fun and also the pain of designing with living things is that they change over the years. Plants grow and shade out adjacent plants. Different plants grow at different rates. How to design for that? My solution: where I think the conditions will change through the day or over the years, I choose plants that will be happy in sun as well as shade. For intensely sunny spots (that will remain so) I choose the sunbathers, and for the deep shade, I choose the delicate ones that would fry in the sun. For everything else, I choose those nonpicky plants, the part-sun/part-shade ones.

Above all, don't stress! Keep in mind that this planting plan is your best shot, but it is by no means final. As plants grow at different rates (or not at all what it said on the label), look stressed out where they are planted, or look terrible together, you, the gardener, will move them around. It is a living work of art, and that is the fun part.

Make your final plant list

From your planting plan you can draw up a nursery shopping list. You will need to count how many of each plant you have specified. To do this, put tracing paper over your planting plan and mark off each mass as you enter the name and quantity of plants on your worksheet 8. This will be your final plant list. Also note the size of container you plan to purchase (4-inch, 1-gallon, 2-gallon, and 5-gallon containers are standard for perennials and shrubs; 5-gallon and 15-gallon containers are standard for trees).

Alternatively, you may choose to forego this last step and simply have a list for each microclimate of your yard, which you can refer to as you add plants over time to your naturescape.

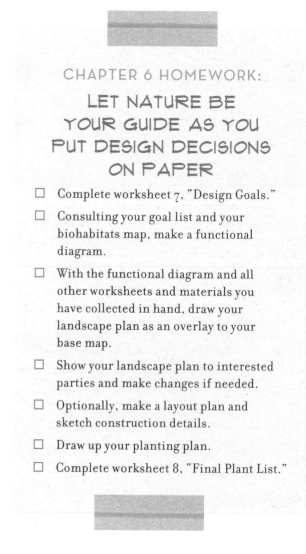

CHAPTER 6 HOMEWORK:

LET NATURE BE YOUR GUIDE AS YOU PUT DESIGN DECISIONS ON PAPER

☐ Complete worksheet 7, "Design Goals."

☐ Consulting your goal list and your biohabitats map, make a functional diagram.

☐ With the functional diagram and all other worksheets and materials you have collected in hand, draw your landscape plan as an overlay to your base map.

☐ Show your landscape plan to interested parties and make changes if needed.

☐ Optionally, make a layout plan and sketch construction details.

☐ Draw up your planting plan.

☐ Complete worksheet 8, "Final Plant List."

Repeating masses of black-eyed Susan, lamb's ears, and variegated iris lends unity to this naturalistic tableau. Their forms contrast for added interest. A purple butterfly bush adds a color contrast. Design by Karen Bussolini.

WORKSHEET 8: FINAL PLANT LIST

LIST EVERY PLANT SHOWN ON YOUR PLANTING PLAN, FOLLOWING THE EXAMPLE SHOWN HERE.

PLANT	QTY	SIZE
Rudbeckia fulgida (black-eyed Susan)	26	1 gal.

PLANT	QTY	SIZE

chapter seven

FROM THE GROUND UP

Think in terms of whole systems as you install your naturescape, from clearing the land to planting and mulching.

Grab your planting plan: it's time to take it outside. You've now reached the enthralling step where all your research, planning, and sketching is going to pay off as you put your shovel in the dirt and transform your yard into the naturescape of your dreams. This chapter takes you through the entire installation sequence in detail. You will be encouraged to think in terms of whole systems as you clear your land, amend the soil in your planting beds, build the hardscape, and plant and mulch. The naturescaping way is to keep materials on the land whenever possible, turn waste into inputs, and dispose of anything you can't use in an environmentally responsible manner.

You can install your naturescape bit by bit as you have the time and money, or you can install it all at once if that works for you. Every project, big or small, piecemeal or entire, is constructed in the same basic sequence. Landscape contractors have this sequence down cold. They can look at a yard and a plan and write out a list of what needs to be done when, along with what manpower, tools, and supplies need to be on site on any given day. It sounds daunting, but I would encourage you to do the same. Create your own installation checklist (worksheet 8) as you make your way through this chapter and determine what needs to be done in your particular case. Jot down target dates and check items off as you complete them.

WORKSHEET 9: INSTALLATION CHECKLIST

1. WHAT I NEED TO DO TO CLEAR THE LAND:

DONE

☐

☐

☐

☐

2. WHAT I NEED TO LAY OUT IN CHALK OR PAINT:

DONE

☐

☐

☐

☐

3. MY PLAN FOR AMENDING THE SOIL:

DONE

☐

☐

☐

☐

4. HARDSCAPE ELEMENTS TO INSTALL:

DONE

☐

☐

☐

☐

5. MY PLAN FOR PLANTING AND MULCHING THE BEDS, AND INSTALLING THE LAWN (IF ANY):

DONE

☐

☐

☐

☐

Clear the Land

One hallmark of the naturescaping approach to installation is keeping materials on the land, realizing that there is really no "away" to throw elements you remove. So keep that thought in mind as you have at all those things that have been bothering you—that rusty gate, the half-dead tree, the planting bed and fence smothered in ivy, the water-gulping lawn, the field of brambles. Clearing the land is sweaty but satisfying work. You're giving yourself a blank slate to work with, at least in the part of your garden you've decided to renovate. Of course, if you're installing a new garden on a bare lot, you can skip this task.

Instead of installing your naturescape all at once, you may want to focus on one small area at a time, like this side yard that the homeowner made over with shade-loving perennials, ferns, and shrubs.

Relocate plants

You will need to save the plants that will be part of the new garden, just not at their present location. It's difficult to tell if something will survive if transplanted, but if it was originally planted within the last five years, you might want to try. Also, if the root-ball is small enough that you can move most of it, it might transplant okay. There are no guarantees, but if you choose a mild day, or a mild part of the day (in the 60s F would be preferable), and plant and water it right away, it will have a better chance of survival.

Here's how to do it: dig up most, if not all, of the root-ball, shake off the nonclinging soil, and set it aside. Dig a hole wider than the root-ball and leave the excavated soil in a pile. To that soil add and gently mix in a bit of aged compost. Put the root-ball into the hole, oriented the same direction as it was before, if possible, and backfill with the soil-compost mix, tamping the soil lightly so as to increase root-soil contact. Create a basin around the transplant so that water stays there rather than running off (on a hillside, this will look like a little terrace; that's fine). Water thoroughly in order to settle the soil.

If you are not able to plant the transplant immediately and if the root-ball is small enough to fit it into a pot, put it in a plastic pot (it would dry out too quickly in a clay pot). Don't cut a lot of roots to make it fit, though. For larger root-balls (or if you don't have pots), simply put the entire root-ball into a plastic bag (a grocery bag or larger). It may sound tacky, but I know an expert gardener who moved her entire yard this way. Leave the bag a little bit open at the top, just enough to let the roots breathe but not dry out. The plant can keep a few days—even weeks, but that might lower its chance of survival—this way if you are careful to keep it moist but not waterlogged.

If your transplant needs to be out of the ground longer than a few days, you may want to "heel it in"—that is, plant it temporarily in a light sawdust/dirt mix. If you choose to do this, make sure the transplant is protected from drying winds and hot, direct sun even though it might naturally be a sun-lover, since it is already under stress.

GARDEN ORNAMENTS AND STRUCTURES: SHOULD IT STAY OR SHOULD IT GO?

KEEP IT IF...

- It enhances your life.
- It brings you enjoyment.
- It serves a purpose in your yard.

CONSIDER GIVING IT AWAY IF...

- You would prefer it were not there.
- It blocks a good view.
- It needs repair or maintenance that you are unwilling to do (be honest with yourself about this).
- It could be reused as something useful or pretty.
- Another person or group could benefit from having it.

THINK REUSE

Rather than throwing something you've taken apart into the dumpster, consider that you are moving it into its next life. Can someone else use it?

- Put it by the curb with a "free" sign.

- List it on a local want-ad website, such as http://www.freecycle.org or http://www.craigslist.org.

- Cut it up and use it as something else. For example, broken-up concrete can be repurposed to create stack-stone walls or relaid upside down to create a rustic driveway.

- Check with the local woodworkers' guild if you need to cut down an exotic tree—they might be interested in the wood and willing to cut it down for you.

- Offer wood from removed trees to churches, gleaners, or other nonprofits that might want to cut it into firewood or starter sticks to distribute to its needy members.

- Cut old fencing materials into firewood—but only if the wood is untreated. Do not burn treated wood in your fireplace or wood stove.

- Give away smaller plants you don't want to friends or to a garden club.

- Better yet, have the club come to you—some clubs have "digging parties" where they will come and pot up your plants for their next fund-raiser plant sale.

If it might contain leachfield contaminants—the case with old railroad ties and varnished wood—call your waste disposal facility to learn how to dispose of these things safely.

Want it gone quickly? Put it out by your curb with a "free" sign.

Lawn be gone

If you have decided to reduce your thirsty, demanding lawn to a patch small enough to mow with a push mower, the naturescaping way is to remove it without using herbicides. There are a few effective ways to do this that also keep the material on your land, so the lawn actually decomposes and feeds the soil.

One is the upside-down lawn. First, mow the lawn to near-baldness. Then pull up portions of the lawn with a sod cutter (these can be rented) or a sturdy square-nosed shovel and place them upside down where you intend future planting beds to be, roots and soil for all to see. Slowly, the roots will dry out and the grass will smother from lack of oxygen and photosynthesis; this organic matter will eventually rot down and enrich your soil.

Smothering with cardboard and mulch is another tried-and-true method to eliminate or reduce your lawn. This is best done when the air moisture level will be high in the next few months, as in the fall. Take pieces of cardboard and place them on top of the grass you want to kill, with some overlap so the sun doesn't get in between the cracks. This can also be done with newspaper sections (ten to twenty pages per section), but only if the ink is soy- or vegetable-based. Try not to use glossy, colored newspaper because the inks are most likely not soy-based. Then add a thick—6 inches at least—layer of organic mulch. Fallen leaves are perfect for this, which is a good reason to do this in the fall. Soak it with a hose (or let a rainstorm do the soaking for you) and leave it for a few months, undisturbed, so the worms and microbes can do their magic. Dig into the leaves after a few months and you might find some nice soil, ready for planting. (This may take longer if you live in an arid climate).

If you are into quicker gratification, it's summer, and the part of your lawn you want gone gets at least four hours of strong midday sunlight a day, solarization is for you. Solarizing your lawn is, simply, frying your lawn. Start by mowing the area within an inch of its life and then saturate the ground with water to a depth of at least 12 inches. Place big sheets of black plastic (clear also works) over the grass you want dead and weigh down the edges with boards to keep a tight seal. The sheets have to be large (more than 5 feet square) so it gets really hot under there; small sheets make the lawn uncomfortable but not to the point of giving up the ghost. Leave the plastic in place for six weeks or so.

Waste the weeds

Weeds also need to be removed, from the questionable ones ("Is it a weed? It has such a pretty flower!") to the merely annoying ones (the uninvited guests) to the tenacious invasives—the Himalayan blackberries, the kudzu, the English ivy. Again, the naturescaping way is not to resort to herbicides. Dig them up by hand as much as possible.

For tenacious invasives, your best bet is to seek out your state's cooperative extension publications for advice on how to best rid your yard of them permanently. If you don't find the information you need there, look up the extension publications for adjacent states (invasives don't respect state boundaries). Another best bet: talk to local gardeners. The emphasis here is on *local*; a solution you might find online in an archival gardening chatroom posting might be effective where that gardener lives but useless in your neighborhood.

Don't try to compost invasives or weeds that have gone to seed: the seeds or root segments might survive the process. Some municipalities pick up yard waste separately and convert that to compost. If they use a hot-compost method (and they should by law if they are selling or giving away the compost), it would be all right to give them your weeds; otherwise, don't. If you have no other options, put the weeds in with your landfill-bound garbage, but only as a last resort since any once-living thing put into a landfill contributes to production of methane, which is a very damaging greenhouse gas.

And remember that weeds love bare ground, especially if it is in the sun. After you have removed all of your unwanteds, cover any exposed soil with a mulch of some sort to keep new weeds from popping up. Ideally you will be adding organic matter, but rocks or even cardboard will do the trick.

Lay It Out

When you've cleared the land and have a blank slate, it's time to mark your layout on the ground. Go to your local hardware store or garden center and get some powdered marking chalk or field paint (used for marking athletic fields). Using your landscape plan (or, if you made one, your layout plan) as your guide, mark key points that will enable you to draw the layout on the ground. Here's how to do this:

1. Make a baseline by stretching out a measuring tape aligned exactly with one wall of the house, just like you did when you were measuring your yard.

2. Referring to your plan, mark dots at the exact points where edges of paths, lawns, planting beds, or other features cross the baseline. For example, where one side of a path crosses the baseline, say 6 feet from the corner of the house, put a dot of paint or chalk. Where the lawn edge crosses the baseline, say 12 feet 6 inches from the house corner, put another dot.

Save those leaves to pile on top of lawn you want to smother.

3. Eventually, when you have enough dots, connect them with a line of paint or chalk (eyeball this), and you will start to see the fence lines, the patio, the decks, the paths, and the lawn edges (or whatever is included in your layout plan) emerge.

4. Add every feature as a rough outline. For example, you would not need to draw the details of a play structure; simply showing the outline of the soft landing material around the structure would be enough. The important thing is that everything is outlined to scale and exactly where it will go.

Exactly may be too strong a word. After all, this is fieldwork, and everything changes in the field. You might encounter a big ugly slab of concrete under some weeds where a beautiful fern garden was supposed to go, or later on, a massive root where a posthole is needed. If you find something like this, just make the adjustments you need to make and try to note it on your plans because it may affect the quantities and locations of the plants.

Build Your Soil

Your next task is to amend the soil where there will be planting beds or lawn. Because this is a naturescape, you will be doing it organically and with great appreciation for soil as the foundation of all life. My friend James, the soil scientist, says "Soil is it, man! The alpha and the omega, where everything starts and where it all ends. It feeds the world. We need to show it more respect." He's right, of course. In our home gardens we destroy delicate soil structures with our rototillers and shovels, kill the soil life with pesticides, rake up and discard nutritious organic matter, and expose the bare soil to the elements. We need to make amends. Luckily, the soil is quite forgiving and will come back to life with a few seasons of good stewardship.

Soil is an incredible system and we know so little about it—renowned biologist E. O. Wilson estimates that we know less than 3 percent of the creatures in soil, and much less than that about

Mark your layout with marking chalk or field paint, available at hardware stores.

their intricate interactions—but we do know that it works. Soil starts as broken-down rock fragments—minerals, in other words (clay soil is a little different, but let's just go with that). Between those rock fragments are air pockets. In some of those air pockets are bits and pieces of organic matter (anything that was once alive, or a product of something alive) in varying levels of decay. Eating and excreting this, and each other, are tiny living creatures. They do a fine job of breaking their food into basic chemicals; nitrogen, phosphate, and magnesium are just a few. If soil contains all of the above—that is, if there are minerals, air pockets, nutritious organic matter, water, creatures, and broken-down chemicals—the soil is said to have good structure and a healthy soil food web.

Unless your yard has been an organic farm or a stable for the last fifty years, it's a safe bet that the soil in your planting beds could benefit from some amending so that it will be a welcoming medium for your new plants. At this point in the installation process, it's time to decide how you will amend your soil—and do it.

Add compost

The best way to amend soil is to mix compost into the top few inches and then top it with a weed-resistant mulch immediately after planting. (More on the mulch later.) Compost is simply organic material that has been completely digested so that it has no smell and does not resemble the parent material at all. Quality compost contains no substances toxic to plants, nonorganic materials, weeds, or viable seeds; it smells like good dirt. Although compost looks like soil, it is not; it contains no sand, silt, or clay particles. It is created by combining organic wastes—such as yard trimmings, food wastes, and manures—and accelerating the decomposition process by controlling temperature, moisture, and oxygen levels. In this way, waste products become inputs in the whole system that is your naturescape.

Compost is available commercially, or you can make it yourself. Increasingly, municipalities are creating compost from the yard debris they collect each week and selling it back to the community.

You can add compost to the soil any time of year that the earth is showing and that you can get out there with a shovel. You can put 2 to 3 inches of it on top of the soil or incorporate (till) it into the top few inches.

This brings us to the till/no-till controversy of the garden world. Advocates on the "till" side argue that tilling compost into the soil gets the nutrition and organic material where it is needed—down by the roots. The "no-till" side argues that tilling breaks up established corridors and relationships within the soil. Both sides agree, for the most part, that tilling with a machine (such as a rototiller) should be done sparingly and shallowly, if at all.

HOW COMPOST IMPROVES ANY SOIL

- The soil can withstand compaction better because of the microscopic tunnels and holes that absorb the pressure and then bounce back, like a sponge.

- Compost increases the nutrient-holding capacity of the soil, improving root growth and plant health.

- The additional nutrients (added as well as created as a result of the compost) protect plants from disease and insect attacks and eliminate the need for synthetic fertilizers.

- The nooks and crannies created when the decomposers are at work improve water retention and increase a plant's tolerance to drought, while also increasing ease of cultivation for the gardener.

- Increased microbial and earthworm populations contribute to the food chain.

MAKE YOUR OWN COMPOST

Making your own compost is an easy way to recycle yard and kitchen waste. You know what is in the compost you spread on your soil, and you save on trucking "waste" away and compost in. You are also reducing greenhouse gas production, and not only because the compost is local. Organic material decomposing anaerobically in a landfill produces methane, which is twenty-three times more potent than carbon dioxide in trapping heat in our atmosphere.

Everything living eventually becomes compost, so it should not be very difficult to create it. Simply start a pile of organic stuff—lawn clippings, manure, newspaper, coffee grounds, kitchen scraps, leaves, weeds (if not invasive and if they haven't yet gone to seed), dead plants—in an out-of-the-way corner of your garden and keep adding to it. Eventually, the oldest stuff at the bottom will become compost.

You might want to keep critters from spreading this all over your yard by putting it into a bin of some sort. Using a bin also keeps heat and moisture in the pile so that it cooks better and faster, and protects the pile from hot sun, heavy rain, and wind. The ideal dimensions for a bin or pile are 3 feet by 3 feet by 3 feet. Your bin doesn't need to be elaborate and can be made of old wood pallets (often available for free at businesses that receive a lot of shipments), wire mesh with the corners staked (or bent into a circle), or cinder blocks. There are also plastic composters on the market.

You can speed the process along by having the optimum ratio of brown material (leaves and branches, which supply carbon) to green material (grass clippings and kitchen scraps, which supply nitrogen). The pile will ideally contain two to three times more brown than green materials by volume. Turning the pile periodically (once a week is best, but as often as you can get around to it is better than never turning it) helps decomposition by providing oxygen. Keeping the pile moist—like a wrung-out kitchen sponge—also aids the decomposers. Some people even add worms or—going further still—maintain a worm bin (in which worms are fed kitchen scraps and encouraged to multiply).

Some gardeners claim that a tea made by suspending aged compost in water for a few days, then adding sugar, has the effect when sprayed on the soil of making plants larger, greener, and lusher; suppressing plant diseases; and even acting as a pesticide. Most of the academic community, however, asserts that at best it will improve plant health and at worst it will harbor human pathogens such as *E. coli*, so the jury is still out on this.

Compost bins help speed up the decomposition process and also protect the compost from the elements and marauding animals. Having two bins makes it easier to turn it over periodically.

Plant cover crops

A cover crop is an annual plant that can be turned into the soil after it is spent, thereby adding nutrients. Farmers call it "green manure." For naturescaping purposes, if you will be having bare ground for a season or two, you might want to consider spreading seeds, letting them grow for that season, and then turning the plants back into the soil.

Plants in the pea family (such as clover, lupines, beans, and peas) are considered great cover crops because they fix nitrogen, one of the major nutrients needed for plant health. That is, they take the nitrogen floating around in the soil, unavailable to plants as is, and make it available to plants in a form they can take up. Fava beans and red clover are two of the most popular nitrogen-fixing cover crops.

Legumes make great—and tasty—cover crops. After these peas are harvested, the plants can be turned back into the soil to enrich it. Design by Thyrza Whittemore.

Add individual nutrients?

You may have noticed that there has been no mention of adding fertilizer—organic or synthetic—to improve the soil. This is because with a healthy dose of organic matter, most soils are highly capable of sustaining plant life. If a plant doesn't seem to be doing well in your yard, it may simply need to be moved to a more hospitable site—or it may just be too fussy for your naturescape.

PEAT AS A SOIL AMENDMENT

What about peat moss? This product of bogs in northern lands—primarily Finland, Canada, Ireland, and Sweden—has been touted for years as a great organic soil amendment for home gardens. However, it is becoming clear that all of that peat mining is not good for the environment, as it destroys wildlife habitat and releases carbon dioxide. On the other hand, peat can be a renewable resource and seems to be in ample supply in Canada; the Canadian Sphagnum Peat Moss Association logo on a bag of peat shows that it was harvested from a bog where strict environmental guidelines are in place. But even environmentally correct peat may have to travel too many miles to get to your yard, so favor local materials whenever possible.

Add the Hardscape

It's time to install the hardscape items: any patios, gazebos, decks, paths, lighting—in short, all of the structural parts of your new naturescape. The best time to work on hardscape is in the spring after the ground has thawed and dried out a bit, in the summer, and into the fall until the ground becomes soggy or frozen. You do not want heavy machinery roaring over squishy soil; think of all the microbes below and the healthy air pockets you are eliminating. It takes a long time to heal soil that has been ruined like that. Timing your project with the seasons is the best protection for your soil.

So, if the timing is right, do your hardscape construction projects right after you have cleared the land and amended the soil. If the land is too soggy or frozen, wait a few months until you can do the construction without harming the soil. You might use that time to gather permits, since any construction you are doing might need to be permitted.

To find out, call your local planning or licensing department and tell them what you have in mind. Again, many places have height and setback restrictions in regard to fencing, raised decks, and tall outdoor structures. It is your responsibility to be aware of, and follow, all of these restrictions, codes, and laws. Sometimes subdivisions have rules that your city does not; check your home purchase papers for CC&R's (covenants, codes, and restrictions) to see if there are any that might apply to your property.

Installing the hardscape is the point in naturescaping where it might seem most difficult to do no ecological harm. It might help to consider the advice Toby Hemenway gives in *Gaia's Garden* about the necessity of making ecological compromises. He recommends thinking long term and doing what it takes to get your backyard ecosystem up and running, even if that includes renting a power tiller once or bulldozing to grade a site. "Using nonrenewable resources to create a landscape is justified if in the long run, that landscape will conserve or provide more resources than it took to build it," says Hemenway.

HARDSCAPE CONSTRUCTION GUIDELINES

• Choose your access point(s) carefully. Whether the heaviest equipment you will need to bring on-site is a wheelbarrow or a tractor, try to make your access point(s) and paths where, in the final design, nothing will be growing (such as a patio, deck, or walkway).

• When you've chosen the access point(s), protect the soil from compaction with boards or rocks (for heavy machinery) or with plywood or sawdust (for pedestrian access).

• Protect your trees. Contractors put orange netting around the dripline (the edge of the canopy, projected onto the ground) of large trees on a job site. You might want to do the same and not step into that area or store any equipment there.

• Work back to front. If possible, start with the projects farthest from the access point(s), like painting a floor.

• Don't forget the sleeving. Before you lay anything permanent in the soil, like concrete or asphalt, figure out if you will need to have underground irrigation or electric lines crossing it. If so, add 4-inch pipe that won't corrode where those lines will go before you pour the concrete or asphalt.

DO YOU NEED PROFESSIONAL HELP?

You might feel like you were never meant to lay concrete pavers or fell big trees. If that is the case, there are people to help you. But before you pick up the phone and randomly call contractors, do a little homework. The best thing you can do is walk around your neighborhood or town and notice if there is a bit of work—an arbor, a driveway—that you really like. Screw up your courage, ring the doorbell, and ask who did that beautiful work. If it was the person who answers the door, you have made a friend for life. If the homeowner had a contractor, ask for the name, as well as how much it cost, how long it took, and how reliable and easy to work with the contractor was.

How can you tell if the contractor will be on board for a naturescape and all that entails? Many contractors these days advertise themselves as green, and some legitimately are. But as of this writing, there are no tests, credentials, or certifications to prove that the contractor actually goes by this philosophy. If the contractor claims to be certified in some way, make sure that it is backed by a legitimate environmental group, preferably one that you have heard of. The best way to measure whether a contractor is a good fit, of course, is by talking to him or her about what you have in mind.

So make the call. Don't indicate that the contractor was recommended by someone or you might get a high bid. Of course, make sure the contractor is licensed and ask for the license number. You can go online or call your state contractor's board and find out things such as how long the contractor has been in the business and if any complaints have been filed or disciplinary actions taken against her or him in the last few years.

Plant and Mulch

With all that amended soil waiting in beds and with pathways installed, your naturescape is finally ready for planting. But when is the best time to plant? Where can you find the native plants on your plant list, and what should you look for when you go to the nursery? What provisions should you make for irrigating your newly installed plants? How do you finish off your planting beds in a way that recycles waste into inputs and builds your soil over time?

To every thing, there is a season

Take a cue from nature about the best times to plant. Working in harmony with natural forces takes a lot less energy than going against them. You definitely want to avoid planting anything during the hottest part of the summer and during the midwinter when the ground is frozen or saturated. The former is hard on you (the waterer) and the plants, and the latter is hard on you (the digger) and the soil.

In general, fall is the best time to plant trees, shrubs, and perennials from containers so that the roots have time to develop over the winter months before spring's burst of growth. You can also get trees, berries, and roses with bare roots in early winter and plant as soon as the ground has thawed, or right away in mild-winter climates; these cost less and get established more quickly than if you planted them from containers in spring. If you miss the fall planting window, the next best time to plant container trees, shrubs, and perennials is spring, but in some regions you won't have the advantage of winter precipitation to keep the roots happy and will probably need to haul some water.

Seeds for cover crops, wildflowers, grass, or lawn substitutes like Dutch white clover are best sown in late fall (when, in nature, the seeds are dropping to the ground and the sky starts providing moisture). Annuals, and some fall-blooming bulbs, are best planted in the spring. If you are in doubt, ask at the nursery or your local cooperative extension office, or refer to your state's extension publications.

PLANT WITH THE SEASONS

SUMMER

fall vegetables, from seed or starts

FALL

container trees, shrubs, and perennials

wildflower, cover crop, and grass or lawn-substitute seeds

spring-blooming bulbs

fall vegetables, from seed or starts

WINTER

bare-root trees, berries, and roses

vegetable seeds (indoors)

SPRING

container trees, shrubs, and perennials

annuals

fall-blooming bulbs

summer vegetables, from seed or starts

Plants should be put in the ground as soon after bringing them home from the nursery as possible. With your planting plan in hand, you might even dig the holes before you go to the nursery. The last thing you want to do is become a slave to watering your nursery containers for weeks while you get the holes ready—or even worse, let them die while you decide where to put them. That's why you've planned the layout in advance and have a plant list to take to the nursery with you.

At the nursery

Take a copy of your plant list to nurseries in your area. Ask if they would be able to fulfill your plant list—or special-order plant stock they don't carry. If your list is on your computer, could you e-mail it to them? See if the nursery has a healthy selection of native plants and maybe even a display encouraging their use. And finally, would they give you a quantity discount? Chances are, if they see that big juicy plant list, they will. Ask for 10 percent, or even more if you are brave; the worst they can do is say no!

Here is what you should look for in nursery stock:

❧ **Trees and shrubs have been given room to breathe.** Signs that they have been squished together: one side of the plant is fuller than the other, there are bare spots, branches have no lower growth.

❧ **Roots are neither swimming in a sea of dirt nor crowded.** Stick a finger in the pot to see how loose the soil is. If you can tell that the root-ball is tiny, you know that it has just been repotted—and tagged with a higher price. Conversely, if it's difficult to get your finger in, the plant has been in that pot for too long. You might be getting a bargain (a big plant in a small pot), but if the roots are very old, circling the pot, and won't break apart with some gentle prying, it's not worth it. A good nursery has a repotting schedule that keeps the roots in enough soil so they are always putting out new little roots.

❧ **The soil in the pots is dark and fresh looking, without big chunks of wood chips, Styrofoam, or other nonsoil additives.**

Sale plants are sometimes a bargain, sometimes not. If a sale plant looks pretty good and is on your plant list, by all means buy it. It's easy for retail nurseries to overstock and miscalculate the demand; why shouldn't you benefit from this? Perennials in the fall when they are not looking so hot are also a great bargain if they are on your plant list. You know they are going to look great next summer.

Bare-root or balled-and-burlapped plants are also a great bargain. These are trees and shrubs that are pulled out of the soil and sold during the plant's dormant season. Don't be put off by the dead look of them; once they are in your yard they will take off and be blooming in no time.

HOW TO PLANT A TREE, SHRUB, OR PERENNIAL

Start by digging a hole as deep as the pot and twice as wide. Gently pull the plant out of the pot and shake out the extra soil, letting it fall into the pile of dug-out soil. Try to pull away the roots so they are not circling the plant. If the roots are tightly wound, you might want to gently rinse the roots to help pull them apart. Don't get too rough, though; the tiny rootlets are how the plant will be getting its water and nutrients for the next few weeks (until it grows more).

Put the plant in the middle of the hole with the roots fanning out and the "collar" (the soil level when it was in the pot) slightly higher than the surrounding soil. Mix the backfill soil with a bit of aged compost, if you have it, and the pot soil. Do not overdo it with the compost, however; if the backfill is too rich, the roots won't venture into the undisturbed soil but will instead circle, stunting the plant's growth, sometimes dramatically.

Put this mix back into the hole, leaving a nice large moat, 2 to 3 feet in diameter, around the collar of the plant so that when you water (deeply and infrequently, which means every week or so), the water will stay in the moat rather than run off, and plenty of water will sit around the plant for a few minutes before percolating into the root zone. Water the plant deeply, while gently pushing down the soil around the plant with your foot so that the roots have good contact with the soil, and repair the moat as needed. Cover the soil with one to two inches of mulch.

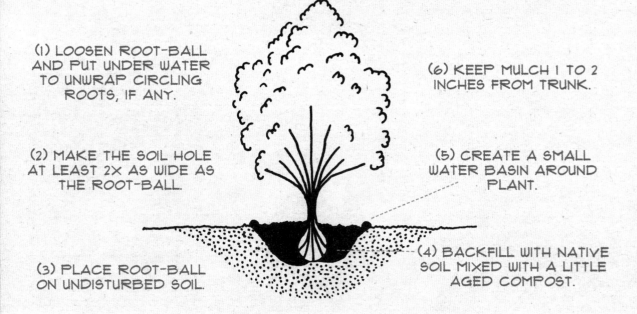

(1) LOOSEN ROOT-BALL AND PUT UNDER WATER TO UNWRAP CIRCLING ROOTS, IF ANY.

(2) MAKE THE SOIL HOLE AT LEAST 2X AS WIDE AS THE ROOT-BALL.

(3) PLACE ROOT-BALL ON UNDISTURBED SOIL.

(6) KEEP MULCH 1 TO 2 INCHES FROM TRUNK.

(5) CREATE A SMALL WATER BASIN AROUND PLANT.

(4) BACKFILL WITH NATIVE SOIL MIXED WITH A LITTLE AGED COMPOST.

How to plant. Stakes are not recommended unless the plant wants to lean or wind is a problem; monitor and remove stakes when they are no longer needed.

Crushed oyster shells are a natural mulch that has been used since George Washington's day.

Optionally install drip irrigation

If you live in an area where it gets so hot and dry that your plants might need watering once in a while, or if your yard is simply too large for hand watering, you may want to use soaker hoses or aboveground drip irrigation lines. After you have planted everything but before you cover it all with a nice blanket of mulch is the time to lay these lines. Snake the soaker hoses among the beds, making sure that each plant is touched, or nearly touched, by the hose. For drip irrigation, lay the hard lines directly on the soil surface and run each spaghetti line to the plants.

Mulch the planting beds

After you've put all your plants in the ground, add a 2-to-6-inch layer of mulch in all of the planting beds, except seedbeds that might need a little more air access. This will protect the young, some-what traumatized roots of your plants, keep in the soil moisture, and make the yard look finished. It will improve your soil over time, just like adding compost does. It will also help you keep waste materials on your land and make them into soil inputs.

Mulch is any material spread evenly over the surface of the soil to enhance the growth of plants. Ideally, mulch should also improve the appearance of the landscape. Note that mulch does not have to be organic (that is, once having been alive). Rocks qualify as mulch because of their ability to keep the soil from drying out, to regulate soil temperature (absorb excess heat when it is sunny and radiate it back into the soil when the sun goes down), and act as a barrier to weeds. Sheets of black plastic can also be considered a mulch, as long as they allow moisture to enter and escape the soil, but they don't exactly improve the appearance of the landscape.

For the most part, though, people are thinking *organic* when they think mulch. Organic mulch is anything that was once living—wood and bark, straw and grass, dead bugs and seashells. Almost any organic material that does not have potentially toxic components (such as hay treated with an herbicide) can be mulch. The best organic mulch, in my opinion, is fallen leaves. That's because they are free, plentiful at a certain time of year, nearby, and ready—meant—to break down and feed the organisms below. Leave the leaves; let them fall in the fall.

MATERIALS THAT CAN SERVE AS MULCH

newspapers (covered with something else to look better and stay down)

chopped garden waste

grass clippings (in a thin layer so they turn brown within a few hours)

leaves

sawdust

straw

grain elevators' chaff and cleanings

alfalfa pellets

ruined hay

tobacco stems

seaweed

mint compost

buckwheat hulls

nutshells

pine needles

wood chips, aged at least one year (fresh chips rob soil of nitrogen)

aged manure (no smell)

old wool blankets and carpets

shredded love letters

Christmas tree limbs

crushed seashells

When you mulch your soil, the worms and microorganisms do all of the heavy lifting. You provide the food and they go up to the surface for the goodies, creating air pockets and aerating the soil like nothing else can (and leaving behind a trail of nutrient-rich castings). They bring the food down, bit by bit, deep into the soil, where it is consumed and decomposes, feeding multitudes of microbial creatures that multiply amidst such plenty. The movement of these creatures aerates the soil, and their castings and dead bodies are consumed by still more creatures. Eventually the soil fauna break down all of the organic materials to basic chemicals—fertilizers—ready to be sucked up by the plant roots. The result is a nutritious and pleasant milieu (all those water molecules and air pockets) for healthy plant growth.

Organic mulch improves *any* soil texture—from fast-draining sand to moisture-retentive silt and clay and everything in between. In sandy soil, the mulch allows the creatures to build pockets of water-retaining organic material between the particles. In clay or silt, the same happens, and the organic material holds water, which pushes apart the clay and silt particles. In pretty good soil, known as loam (a mixture of sand, silt, and clay), it just makes everything better. While encouraging all of this microbial activity, mulch also protects the top layer of soil from temperature extremes, from drying out in the sun, and from blowing away in the wind. It keeps out weeds and makes the ones that land on it easy to pluck. What's not to love?

There are some plants you may not want to use as mulch, however. These are the allelopaths, the plants that contain chemicals that prevent other plants from growing near them—the plant equivalent of that guy with the spiked chariot spokes in Ben Hur. It is widely known among gardeners that the black walnut tree (*Juglans nigra*) is allelopathic. Others allelopaths, according to limited studies (in which specific parts of the allelopathic plant affect certain plant species), are the butternut tree

(*Juglans cinerea*), eucalyptus, red maple (*Acer rubrum*), tree-of-heaven (*Ailanthus*), box elder (*Acer negundo*), mango, swamp chestnut oak (*Quercus michauxii*), sweet bay, chaste tree (*Vitex agnus-castus*), red cedar, wheat, rye, lantana, and broccoli. Just to be safe, avoid using hulls, bark, leaves, or chipper mulch made from any of these. (Because compost breaks down the plants more completely, these would most likely be just fine for composting).

CHAPTER 7 HOMEWORK:
THINK IN TERMS OF WHOLE SYSTEMS AS YOU INSTALL YOUR NATURESCAPE

☐ Complete worksheet 9, "Installation Checklist."

☐ Remove unwanted hardscape and plants, including lawn, and aim to keep materials on the land, make waste into inputs, or dispose of items responsibly.

☐ Build the soil in the planting beds with compost (preferably made at home, recycling wastes) and cover crops.

☐ Install the hardscape when the soil is dry.

☐ Plant with the seasons and add mulch to top off your beds.

Fallen leaves are liquid gold. Leave them where they fall, and the soil underneath will become healthier and healthier over time.

chapter eight

STEWARD YOUR NATURESCAPE

Continue to build your soil with organic matter as you maintain your naturescape, for fewer pests and diseases, less watering, and less work.

To steward is to be "morally responsible for the careful use of . . . resources, especially with respect to the principles or needs of a community or group," according to Webster's. Naturescapers use resources carefully—in a caring manner—because we feel morally responsible to live up to the principles of the biggest community of all, the earth, and the biggest group, all living creatures. With those thoughts in mind, let's go over the basics of caring for your naturescape—in other words, being a good steward of your land. In this chapter you will learn about good watering techniques, organic lawn care, pruning for plant health, and what to do when plant diseases and weeds show up.

As you maintain your garden, the most important thing you can do is to continue to build the soil with organic matter. Over time, this will increase the health of your plants so that you will have fewer pests and diseases to contend with and fewer weeds. It will also improve the water-holding capacity of the soil so that you will need to do less and less watering.

Water Efficiently

Because you now have a garden designed to reduce your need for supplemental water, your water bill should eventually go down. However, you may need to water your plants for the first few dry seasons (if you have a dry season). This is especially true for nursery-container plants that were root-bound (had more roots than soil) or had circling, damaged, or rotted roots; these poor things will need time to grow a root system to support their foliage.

Once your plants are established, however, you will probably be able to get by with hand watering or placing sprinklers, if you need to water at all. If your yard is too big for this, you may have decided to place soaker hoses or drip irrigation lines.

To promote deep root growth (which uses less water in the long run), water deeply and infrequently. To make sure the water goes deep into each plant's root zone, create a moat around each plant so water is held for a few minutes before percolating into the soil. This will keep the water from flowing over the soil or between the layer of mulch and soil. To water infrequently, experiment: see how long a plant (or area) can go without wilting and make note of it. Of course, this measurement will not be absolute—one hot, sunny, windy day will shorten the between-watering time significantly— but it is a start. You might be surprised how long some of your plants can go without water.

If you must use sprinklers, water in the morning before it gets very hot so the water goes into the root zone instead of the atmosphere. In August in the western college town where I live, more and more homes in my neighborhood are sporting brown front lawns. Allowing lawn to go dormant in the summer has become socially acceptable—even commendable—in this neighborhood. Still, it was not always this way; a few years back, all the lawns were green (or trying to be). Then one went brown, then another. Could you be the first on your block to let your lawn go brown?

TO HAND WATER EFFICIENTLY

- Water in the evening or early morning to minimize evaporation.
- Direct the watering spout at the base of the plant.
- Water until it begins to run off the surface.
- Return in thirty minutes to an hour to give a second drink for half the time.
- Water only every few days.

Drought-tolerant lamb's ears, lavender, and euphorbia have replaced lawn in this front yard, dramatically cutting its water needs. These plants need supplemental water only while getting established.

THE NATURESCAPER'S TOOLSHED

You will need to invest in some equipment to help nature along. Spend the extra bucks to get the best and most durable. Make sure the metal and the welds are strong. The best way to find top-quality brands is to look into an old gardener's truck. Long ago, he (or she) gave up on the brands that don't last. What's in that truck is only the best.

HERE ARE MY MUST-HAVES:

❧ A push or reel lawn mower. On average, mowing the lawn for one hour with a gasoline-powered mower produces as much pollution as driving 650 miles. Just don't do it.

❧ As an alternative, an electric grasscycling lawn mower. Using electricity is much cleaner (and quieter) than using a carbon-spewing power mower. And one that chews up the grass into tiny, bite-size pieces for the soil fauna below is brilliant.

❧ A chipper/shredder. This is one of those helping-nature-along machines that make naturescaping so much fun. In one day you can prune all the dead wood from your trees and make mulch. (Beware, though—the fresh mulch temporarily sucks the nitrogen out of your soil; better to pile it somewhere for a year before spreading it if this concerns you.)

❧ A propane flamer. There are small flamers made exclusively for weeds. You don't have to create tiny little fires all over your yard, however; a quick go-over usually breaks apart the cell walls enough to ensure a slow, painful death to your (formerly) brazen interlopers. If you have a lot of gravel paths, this is a must-have; otherwise it may not be needed.

❧ A cute little wheelbarrow. Red, of course.

❧ A hula hoe for quick weeding.

❧ A gravel rake (thin, metal tines) to dislodge path weeds before they become big.

❧ A snow shovel for moving around leaves and other natural mulch.

❧ A bamboo rake, not only for raking but also for spreading leaves around your planting beds.

❧ A Japanese garden knife or hori-hori to dig in clay, cut rose bushes, and do other tough jobs.

❧ A Korean hoe, short- or long-handled, to weed and make troughs.

❧ A hand spade, kept sharp, for transplanting small plants.

❧ A pair of sharp hand clippers and a pair of long-handled loppers that can cut branches up to 1-1/2 inches in diameter.

❧ A serrated hand saw for larger cuts.

Get in the habit of rinsing off and drying your tools after a day's work to keep them from rusting. Oil them every once in a while. It is not really necessary to disinfect your tools, since most plant diseases are more likely to be carried by your hands or clothing than your pruning tools.

Care for Your Lawn Organically

The second aspect of good stewardship is organic lawn care. This means practicing an alternative to the norm of spewing polluting chemicals and particles into the air and shattering the peace of the neighborhood with gasoline-powered lawn mowers, leaf blowers, and edgers. Ideally, you've limited your lawn to a size you can comfortably mow with a reel mower. If you need more power, buy a mulching electric mower (or group-buy one for the neighborhood), which is quiet and nonpolluting. These mowers are great for breaking down leaves and twigs for easy composting.

At mowing time, mow high (2 to 3 inches; check with your local cooperative extension office for local recommendations) and mow regularly. When the grass is actively growing, mow frequently enough so that you are cutting only one-third of the height of the grass. Leave the clippings in the grass; spread with a rake if needed. This is called grasscycling.

Far from causing thatch build-up—which is caused by lack of decomposers in the soil— grasscycling aids in thatch breakdown by increasing the number of worms and microorganisms in the soil. The soil organisms recycle the clippings into (free) fertilizer.

Instead of using fertilizer, top-dress your lawn with finely screened compost at least once a year and as much as four times a year. If you do use fertilizer, be aware that slow-release fertilizer, unless it says "organic," is simply synthetic fertilizer with a coating. It may even be touted as "green" and "natural," but neither of those words carry any real meaning. *Organic* is the word you want. Organic fertilizers are, by nature, slow-release. That is, they take some time to break down into the soil.

And for the waterways' sake, sweep up any fertilizer that you accidentally get on your sidewalk, street, or driveway. Fertilizer in streams and rivers causes algae blooms that do real damage to the food web.

This small patch of lawn, intentionally mowed high to preserve moisture in the ground, provides enough space for lawn chairs and is edged with water-conserving perennials such as catmint and lamb's ears.

Prune for Plant Health

I once toured the garden of a friend who was a tree surgeon and noticed that although the plants were not anything out of the ordinary, and in fact were placed rather haphazardly, and although it was a gray March day and not much had leafed out, the word *fresh* came to mind. There were no dead limbs, no crossed limbs; every plant was a sculpture, and every limb had room to breathe. It was the healthiest garden I had ever seen.

Although a well-pruned plant looks great, there are other reasons to keep up with pruning as well. Dead limbs are home to termites and other decomposers, and sometimes they start eating the live bark or enter the wood. It's okay to help the plant along in sloughing off a dead limb—you can leave it elsewhere in the garden so everybody eats. Crossing limbs look bad, but also that sawing motion eventually wears a wound into one or both limbs—a weakened spot perfect for parasites to enter the tree. Careful, surgical removal of crossing limbs is a great way to keep up the plant's health. Regular pruning also saves water (fewer limbs equals less water uptake).

Avoid topping, taking off the top of a tree or shrub like a buzz cut. The remaining limbs will grow back, more plentiful and weaker than any previous limb you cut. In a few years the tree or shrub will be the same size as it was before the butchering, but it will look terrible, like a poodle tail or Dr. Seuss tree. Also avoid heading back or trimming, the euphemism for buzzing all of the outer branches. Know what you are doing first by taking a class, learning from an old pro, or consulting a book like *Pruning Simplified* by Lewis Hill, which covers how to prune virtually every kind of plant you could have, as well as pruning for different uses, such as for fruit production, for transplanting, for rejuvenation, or for aesthetics—all in an easy-to-understand format.

Manage Pests and Diseases Without Chemicals

A few bug-bitten leaves are part of a healthy ecosystem; it means the bugs—and their predators—are getting good food. If you have incorporated plenty of natives in your naturescape, you are providing the native bugs and birds exactly what they need and helping to keep predators and prey in healthy balance. Still, pests and diseases happen, and the best you can do is to manage them without chemicals.

If a plant starts to show signs of stress, disease, or pest problems, first make sure it is getting what it needs in terms of sun-and-wind exposure and water. If nothing is amiss, you might want to simply observe for a few weeks (here's where the hand watering helps; it makes you get out there and notice things). If it is getting worse, it's time to diagnose.

WHEN TO PRUNE

- Prune deciduous trees in the winter before the buds break (that is, when the buds are fat but not opened). The pruning wounds tend to heal quickly in the spring, and there are a lot fewer diseases in the air.

- If you miss that window, prune when you have time, but note the following.

- Prune when the weather is dry, because dry air discourages moisture-borne diseases from spreading.

- If you care about your plants blooming, wait until they have finished blooming before pruning.

- Avoid pruning in late summer because that might stimulate tender new growth that may not have time to harden before the colder weather comes in.

What's Wrong with My Plant? (And How Do I Fix It?) by David Deardorff and Kathryn Wadsworth offers an easy-to-use system of diagnosis and suggests organic solutions. If you are still in doubt after looking it up, your local cooperative extension office would be happy to help if you take a sample of the problem to them. (They have their own reasons for wanting to know if a new disease or pest is in the air—public health and local economies depend on it.) Once you know exactly what it is (correct identification is crucial), you can decide if you want to take action, and if so, which action to take. Then start with the least drastic measure that might remedy the problem.

Sometimes all that is needed is simple husbandry, like moving a plant to a better location or cutting off and hauling away damaged branches. To determine if a limb is dead, any time of year, scratch it and look for green below the bark; if you see none, that part is dead. Continue down the branch until you see some green when you scratch; remove the limb there. If you get down to the trunk and there's no green, it's a goner. Remove it but also try to figure out what killed it (your local extension office can help you with this as well); knowing this will make you a better steward. You may want to rake up and remove diseased leaves from under a sick plant.

If you get a pest problem that is just intolerable to you, like coddling moths in your apples or midnight slug raids that decimate your chard, there are active measures to try once you know exactly what the problem is. Realize that organic pesticides can kill beneficial insects and cause environmental problems just like synthetic ones do, so employ these only as a last resort. For example, the organic pesticide rotenone kills beneficial insects and is potentially harmful to humans.

In The *Truth About Organic Gardening*, Jeff Gillman lists his favorite organic pesticides as *Bacillus thuringiensis* (Bt), diatomaceous earth, and garlic sprays. Bt is species-specific and does not knock out beneficial insect populations. Diatomaceous earth is like tiny shards of glass that ruin the undersides of crawling insects. It is highly effective and not harmful to people unless it is inhaled. Garlic sprays can be made at home and are effective against ticks, aphids, whiteflies, and beetles and not harmful to the beneficials. The fungus *Beauvaria bassiana* is also good if you are trying to rid a plant of aphids, mites, caterpillars, or thrips (and more) and you have wet, humid conditions in which to apply it. Capsaicin, the ingredient in hot peppers, is useful in expelling an insect from a plant without killing it. Insecticidal oils are useful but only if used properly. Of course, all of these insecticides need to be applied exactly as the label directs.

COPPICE TO MANAGE WOODY PLANTS

Coppicing is a form of woodland management that originated thousands of years ago in Europe as a way to sustainably harvest material for fuel, weaving, woodworking, fencing, building, and animal fodder. In a naturescape, coppicing can be a source of kindling wood, building material, and plant supports, and you can also just use it to refresh and restrain shrubby plants. When you coppice a plant, you cut some or all of the stems down to the ground and allow them to regenerate.

Many plants—including redtwig dogwoods, color-stemmed willows, ninebark, weigela, forsythia, butterfly bush, and smokebush—look best with annual coppicing. In late winter or early spring, shorten all stems of vigorous growers like redtwig dogwood and butterfly bush to within a few inches of the ground. For less vigorous growers such as ninebark and forsythia, remove up to half of the old stems every year. Remove only a third of the oldest stems of smokebush each spring to avoid sacrificing flowering.

PEST REMEDIES TO TRY FIRST

Horticultural science professor Jeff Gillman has taken a look at garden remedies and asked what works, what doesn't, and why. Here are a few remedies for pests that he recommends in *The Truth About Garden Remedies*. You can test some of these remedies on a small part of the plant to make sure it does no damage before applying it to the entire plant.

• Control ants by spraying their mounds and trails with a commercial formulation of limonene, a compound found in citrus peel, but avoid spraying on plants.

• Repel whiteflies, aphids, and beetles by spraying plants with a commercially prepared garlic spray or a spray you make yourself by mixing one diced garlic bulb with 2 cups of water, blending thoroughly, straining, and diluting with 1 gallon of water.

• Deter mites and whiteflies by spraying plants with a cayenne pepper solution brewed by adding a few tablespoons of Tabasco to 1 gallon of water.

• Control grubs and crickets by spraying with nematodes, which can be purchased in a dry clay mixture that you add water to.

• Blast aphids and spit bugs off leaves with a strong spray of water.

• Deter tree fruit pests by placing tightly sealed bags around ½-inch fruits on the tree and leaving them on until three weeks before harvest.

• Attract and drown slugs by setting a 6-inch-deep container in the ground with its top level with the soil and filling to within 1 inch of the top with stale beer.

• Reduce pest populations before they get out of hand by releasing purchased insect predators and parasites (available on the Internet) such as lacewings, minute pirate bugs, and parasitic wasps. Gillman does not recommend purchasing ladybugs because they just fly away.

Understand Your Weeds

The commercials tell us that they are bad (and therefore must be eliminated with this spray bottle of death). They look pretty ugly to us. But could they be good? Let's take a look and try to understand the lonely, aggressive, misunderstood weed.

Weeds are successionalists. They are the first step in succession, nature's eternal striving to transition from a disturbed area, such as a landslide, to a thriving, ecologically balanced climax community, such as a stately redwood forest. In this way, weeds are a crucial part of a beautiful ecology.

Weeds are pioneers, the cunning ones who get out there where no other plant wants to be. By hook (Velcro was invented by studying weeds) or by crook (taking free rides on the wind, in water, or even in intestinal tracts), these guys get around. They dig deep into rocky, dry, hard-packed, and/or lifeless soil in amazing feats of survival, most of which we know nothing about. Their roots break up seemingly impenetrable soil, their leaves provide shade, and their carcasses add nutrients to the hungry soil and soil life below. Gradually, the soil rebuilds, becoming more hospitable to the plants we humans find more pleasing, useful, interesting—more refined. As usual, the gentry only survive because of the backbreaking toil of the peasants.

Weeds are good. Without weeds, our really impoverished soils would just blow away, causing incredible dust-bowl effects and leaving us with rocks. But weeds are also cunning and uninvited. Weeds show up in our yards where garden conditions are a bit harsh. There's probably too much sun or the soil is too sandy, clayey, undernourished, or exposed.

Some weeds are just trying to make the world a greener place, like this invasive Himalayan blackberry trying its best to shade a patch of barren ground.

Exotic invasives, like this tree-choking ivy, are bad news and need to be taken sternly in hand.

The naturescaping solution: improve the conditions. Shade the soil with mulch or plants. Improve the soil by adding compost and allowing leaves and other plant debris to stay where it falls. Make your yard less inviting to weeds and they will wander off to the party down the street. It sounds simple, but taking these easy-to-do (and not do, in the case of leaving plant debris) steps will, over time, make your yard nearly weed free. There will always be weeds, but abatement will be much easier: a pleasant afternoon in the garden plucking out the offenders rather than a day of chemical warfare and physical challenges.

On gravel paths, a gravel rake (with narrow metal tines) works great for getting out the little weeds, and the sound is very pleasant. Hula hoes are a fun way to get the more persistent ones. And then there's always flaming: killing weeds with an acetylene torch. If you are so inclined you can flame weeds in concrete or asphalt cracks, in gravel, or even in planting beds. You don't have to send the little guy up in smoke; blackening the base of the plant, leaving it mostly green, does the trick.

But what about the invasive weeds—those aggressive thugs that come into your yard and waste no time growing in and around your invited guests, weakening them and in some cases killing them? Invasives are the criminals of the garden, and they need to be approached with stern measures, up to and including chemicals like glyphosate, the active ingredient in Roundup.

Did I say Roundup? Yes, ecologists have found that in extreme cases, using an herbicide in a very limited manner on these aggressive invaders is the only method that allows native plants to gain a foothold. As one biologist put it, it is like fighting cancer with radiation: it is not harmless; it is a desperate measure taken to save the patient. It is not the best solution, but it is the best we have. (Once the natives gain their ground, the invasives can be held at bay by less dramatic measures: repeated mowing and old-fashioned weed pulling.)

In no way am I suggesting that the first thing you should do is go out and buy plant killers to solve your weed problems. First, observe your weeds: are they successionalists, like dandelions, or invasives, like kudzu? Successionalists can usually be removed by earth-friendly methods. (If you don't know what your weeds are, consult a good weed-identification book or take a sample to your local cooperative extension or soil and water conservation district office.)

If, on the other hand, you have a nasty invader on your land, you might need to resort to chemicals. You might even be obliged to remove the weed by a governmental body, if the weed is threatening local ecosystems or farms. If this is your only solution, do your homework. Make sure the weed is the exact weed you think it is. Then research earth-friendly alternatives to synthetic herbicides. If, as a last resort, you must use an herbicide, learn from trusted experts who are not selling the stuff, such as university professors (through extension publi-

WAYS TO REMOVE SUCCESSIONALISTS

- Hoe the weeds under or away while they are young and the soil is moist.

- Flame the weeds.

- Spray the weeds with cayenne- or clove-based organic weed killers.

- Solarize the weeds by covering with a clear plastic tarp for a few sunny days.

- Turn goats loose in your garden.

cations), what the least environmentally harmful, most effective killer of that particular weed is. Then make sure you purchase only the quantity you need (better yet, buy it from a friend who has it sitting in her garage) and apply according to the label. Also, it would be nice to notify the neighbors with a written note saying what the chemical is, when you will be applying it ("the next calm day" is enough), and where in your yard it will go.

And finally, good garden stewardship starts and ends with good soil. So continually feed your soil with organic material, the way nature does. Once a year in the spring or fall, put a layer of compost or other mulch at least 3 inches deep on top of your beds to keep the moisture in and the weeds down. Compost and mulch—the answer to almost all garden problems. So compost and mulch.

CONTINUE TO BUILD YOUR SOIL WITH ORGANIC MATTER AS YOU MAINTAIN YOUR NATURESCAPE

- ☐ Treat yourself to some high-quality equipment and tools that will make maintaining your naturescape enjoyable.

- ☐ Water efficiently by hand or with a drip or soaker system, tapering off as plants get established.

- ☐ Mow your lawn high, with a reel or mulching mower if possible, and fertilize with compost.

- ☐ Prune out dead and crossing limbs to keep trees and shrubs healthy.

- ☐ Try insecticidal home remedies if a pest is intolerable and regard organic pesticides as a last resort.

- ☐ Identify your weeds and use the most earth-friendly method necessary to eradicate them.

- ☐ At least once a year, put a layer of compost or mulch on your beds.

Above all, take time to use and enjoy your naturescape. Dining al fresco is much more appetizing in a garden of healthy plants. Design by Scott Thurmon.

CONVERSION TABLES

inches	cm		feet	m
1/10	0.3		1	0.3
1/6	0.4		2	0.6
1/4	0.6		3	0.9
1/3	0.8		4	1.2
1/2	1.3		5	1.5
3/4	1.9		6	1.8
1	2.5		7	2.1
2	5.1		8	2.4
3	7.6		9	2.7
4	10		10	3
5	13		20	6
6	15		30	9
7	18		40	12
8	20		50	15
9	23		60	18
10	25		70	21
20	51		80	24
30	76		90	27
40	100		100	30
50	130			
60	150			
70	180			
80	200			
90	230			
100	250			

Temperatures

$$°C = 5/9 \times (°F - 32)$$

$$°F = (9/5 \times °C) + 32$$

Suggested Reading

Alexander, Rosemary. 2009. *The Essential Garden Design Workbook*, 2nd ed. Portland, OR: Timber Press.

Armitage, Allan M. 2006. *Armitage's Native Plants for North American Gardens*. Portland, OR: Timber Press.

Barbarow, Peter. 1990. *Give Peas a Chance! Organic Gardening Cartoon-Science*. Happy Camp, CA: Naturegraph Publishers.

Breskend, Jean. 1998. *Backyard Design: Making the Most of the Space Around Your House*. New York: Bullfinch Press.

Brooklyn Botanic Garden. 2001. *Woodland Gardens: Shade Gets Chic*. Brooklyn, NY: Brooklyn Botanic Garden Publications.

Coleman, Eliot. 1995. *The New Organic Grower: A Master's Manual of Tools and Techniques for the Home and Market Gardener*, 2nd ed. White River Junction, VT: Chelsea Green.

Coleman, Eliot, Barbara Damrosch, and Kathy Bray. 1999. *Four-Season Harvest: Organic Vegetables from Your Home Garden All Year Long*. White River Junction, VT: Chelsea Green.

Deardorff, David, and Kathryn Wadsworth. 2009. *What's Wrong with My Plant? (And How Do I Fix It?): A Visual Guide to Easy Diagnosis and Organic Remedies*. Portland, OR: Timber Press.

DiSabato-Aust, Tracy. 2009. *The Well-Designed Mixed Garden: Building Beds and Borders with Trees, Shrubs, Perennials, Annuals, and Bulbs*. Portland, OR: Timber Press.

Dunnett, Nigel, and Andy Clayden. 2007. *Rain Gardens: Managing Water Sustainably in the Garden and Designed Landscape*. Portland, OR: Timber Press.

Editors of Sunset Books. 1997. *Sunset National Garden Book*. Menlo Park, CA: Sunset Books.

——. 1998. *Western Garden Problem Solver*. Menlo Park, CA: Sunset Publishing.

——. 2010. *Sunset Western Garden Book of Edibles: The Complete A–Z Guide to Growing Your Own Vegetables, Herbs, and Fruits*. Birmingham, AL: Oxmoor House.

Editors of Sunset Books and Kathleen Norris Brenzel. 2007. *Sunset Western Garden Book*, 8th ed. Birmingham, AL: Oxmoor House.

Ferguson, Nicola. 2005. *Right Plant, Right Place: Over 1,400 Plants for Every Situation in the Garden*. New York: Fireside. First ed., Summit Books, 1984.

Gillman, Jeff. 2006. *The Truth About Garden Remedies: What Works, What Doesn't, and Why*. Portland, OR: Timber Press.

——. 2008. *The Truth About Organic Gardening: Benefits, Drawbacks, and the Bottom Line*. Portland, OR: Timber Press.

Greenlee, John. 2009. *The American Meadow Garden: Creating a Natural Alternative to the American Lawn*. Portland, OR: Timber Press.

Halpin, Anne (ed.). 2001. *Sunset Northeastern Garden Book*. Menlo Park, CA: Sunset Books.

Hankinson, Moira, and Nicholas Hankinson. 2001. *Salvage Style for Outdoor Living*. Emmaus, PA: Rodale Press.

Hemenway, Toby. 2009. *Gaia's Garden: A Guide to Home-Scale Permaculture*, 2nd ed. White River Junction, VT: Chelsea Green.

Hill, Lewis. 1986. *Pruning Simplified: A Complete Guide to Pruning Trees, Shrubs, Bushes, Hedges, Vines, Flowers, Garden Plants, Houseplants and Bonsai*. North Adams, MA: Storey Publishing.

Lanza, Patricia. 1998. *Lasagna Gardening: A New Layering System for Bountiful Gardens: No Digging, No Tilling, No Weeding, No Kidding!* Emmaus, PA: Rodale Press.

Levesque, Matthew. 2010. *The Revolutionary Yardscape: Ideas for Repurposing Local Materials to Create Containers, Pathways, Lighting, and More*. Portland, OR: Timber Press.

McGee, Rose Marie Nichols, and Maggie Stuckey. 2002. *The Bountiful Container: Create Container Gardens of Vegetables, Herbs, Fruits, and Edible Flowers*. New York: Workman Publishing.

Messervy, Julie Moir, and Sarah Susanka. 2008. *Outside the Not So Big House: Creating the Landscape of Home*. Newtown, CT: Taunton Books.

Nagel, Vanessa Gardner. 2010. *Understanding Garden Design: The Complete Handbook for Aspiring Designers*. Portland, OR: Timber Press.

Ogden, Scott, and Lauren Springer Ogden. 2008. *Plant-Driven Design: Creating Gardens That Honor Plant, Place, and Spirit*. Portland, OR: Timber Press.

Reich, Lee. 2001. *Weedless Gardening*. New York: Workman Publishing.

Riotte, Louise. 1998. *Carrots Love Tomatoes: The Secret of Companion Planting for Successful Gardening*. North Adams, MA: Storey Publishing.

Robson, Kathleen, Alice Richter, and Marianne Filbert. 2008. *Encyclopedia of Northwest Native Plants for Gardens and Landscapes*. Portland, OR: Timber Press.

Starcher, Allison Mia. 1995. *Good Bugs for Your Garden*. Chapel Hill, NC: Algonquin Books.

Stein, Sara B. 1995. *Noah's Garden: Restoring the Ecology of Our Own Backyards*. Boston, MA: Houghton Mifflin.

———. 1997. *Planting Noah's Garden: Further Adventures in Backyard Ecology*. Boston, MA: Houghton Mifflin.

Sternberg, Guy, with Jim Wilson. 2004. *Native Trees for North American Landscapes*. Portland, OR: Timber Press.

Tallamy, Douglas W. 2009. *Bringing Nature Home: How You Can Sustain Wildlife with Native Plants*. Portland, OR: Timber Press.

Tukey, Paul Boardway. 2007. *The Organic Lawn Care Manual: A Natural, Low-Maintenance System for a Beautiful, Safe Lawn*. North Adams, MA: Storey Publishing.

von Trapp, Sara Jane. 1997. *Landscaping from the Ground Up*. Newtown, CT: Taunton Books.

Williams, Bunny, and Nancy Drew. 1998. *On Garden Style*. New York: Simon & Schuster.

Photography Credits

Andy Hoffman:
pages 37, 107

Lauren Knight:
page 69

Dave Reed:
page 57

Marla Sidrow:
page 24

Ed Snodgrass:
page 61

Larry Thornton:
page 120

Beth O'Donnell Young:
pages 57, 58, 120, 140, 181, 203, 209

Bill Young:
pages 15, 21, 29, 31, 33, 67, 94, 101, 102, 134, 137, 159, 161, 183, 186, 189, 226

All other photographs are by Karen Bussolini.

FSC logo courtesy Forest Stewardship Counsel:
page 147

Index

About the Author

Beth O'Donnell Young is the owner of Beth Young Garden Design, a residential landscape design firm in the Pacific Northwest. She enjoys introducing homeowners to sustainable landscape design and practices through her writings, lectures, and seminars. She has a degree in landscape architecture from U.C. Berkeley.

She currently divides her time between Corvalis, Oregon, and Siena, Italy, where she conducts garden tours, writes, and offers traveler assistance. Beth is lucky enough to be the mother of Liz and Sarah Young.

Beth's website, www.naturescapeyouryard.com, includes downloadable copies of the worksheets in this book.